PENGUIN PASSNOTES

Physics

SUSAN LEE
ADVISORY EDITOR: STEPHEN COOTE, M.A., PH.D.

PENGUIN BOOKS

Penguin Books Ltd, Harmondsworth, Middlesex, England
Viking Penguin Inc., 40 West 23rd Street, New York, New York 10010, U.S.A.
Penguin Books Australia Ltd, Ringwood, Victoria, Australia
Penguin Books Canada Limited, 2801 John Street, Markham, Ontario, Canada L3R 1B4
Penguin Books (N.Z.) Ltd, 182–190 Wairau Road, Auckland 10, New Zealand

First published 1984
Reprinted 1986

Copyright © Susan Lee, 1984
All rights reserved

Made and printed in Great Britain by
Richard Clay (The Chaucer Press) Ltd, Bungay, Suffolk
Filmset in 9 on 10½ pt Monophoto Times by
Northumberland Press Ltd, Gateshead

Except in the United States of America, this book is sold subject
to the condition that it shall not, by way of trade or otherwise, be lent,
re-sold, hired out, or otherwise circulated without the
publisher's prior consent in any form of binding or cover other than
that in which it is published and without a similar condition
including this condition being imposed on the subsequent purchaser

The publishers are grateful to the following Examination Boards for permission to reproduce questions from examination papers used in individual titles in the Passnotes series:

Associated Examining Board, University of Cambridge Local Examinations Syndicate, Joint Matriculation Board, University of London School Examinations Department, Oxford and Cambridge Schools Examination Board, University of Oxford Delegacy of Local Examinations.

The Examination Boards accept no responsibility whatsoever for the accuracy or method of working in any suggested answers given as models.

Contents

1	*Introduction*	7
2	*Exam Technique*	9
	Multiple Choice Papers	9
	Short Answer Questions	12
	Longer Questions	15
3	*Mechanics and Properties of Matter*	18
	Mass, Length, Time, Density, Vectors	18
	Particulate Nature of Matter	25
	Motion in a Straight Line	30
	Laws of Motion	37
	Static Systems	45
	Work, Energy and Power	52
	Machines	56
	Pressure	61
	Flotation	65
	General Questions	71
4	*Heat*	77
	Heat as a Form of Energy. The Kinetic Theory	77
	Measurement of Temperature	81
	Transfer of Thermal Energy	84
	Expansion of Solids and Liquids	89
	Expansion of Gases and the Gas Laws	95
	Specific Heat Capacity	103
	Change of State and Specific Latent Heat	108
	General Questions	112

5   *Waves, Sound and Light*   117

    Vibrations and Waves   117
    Sound   123
    Electromagnetic Waves   130
    Geometric optics   133
        (a) Straight line propagation   133
        (b) Reflection   135
        (c) Refraction   140
        (d) Interference and diffraction   147
    Optical Instruments and Applications   148
    General Questions   155

6   *Electricity and Magnetism*   160

    Power Sources   160
    Currents in Circuits   163
    Elementary Magnetism   170
    Electromagnetic Devices   174
    Electromagnetic Induction   176
    Domestic Electricity Supply   182
    Electrostatics   187
    Moving Charges   190
    The Atom   195
    General Questions   201

Section 1: Introduction

Physics O-level is one of the most popular O-levels, but no one can pretend it is an easy exam to prepare for or to pass. This book is meant to help you, the student, in the way you tackle your preparation and the exam itself, but it is not in any way a substitute for a physics text book or for the teaching you will receive in physics lessons.

The aims of physics O-level courses are set out in most syllabuses. For example, the Joint Matriculation Board (JMB) states:

> Students should derive interest, enjoyment and some sense of achievement from their study of physics ... The syllabus is designed to stimulate an interest in the application of physics, to create opportunities for the discussion of physics-related problems of our time and to inculcate an appreciation not only of the limits of physics but also its achievement in describing the physical world ... This statement is intended to provide a general indication of the abilities which the examination will be designed to test.

However sound these aims may be, they hardly explain how to go about preparing for the exam in detail, and they are not meant to. One of the best ways of doing this preparation is for you to test your own knowledge and understanding to see how thorough they are. A good way is to use past G.C.E. questions, and this book gives you examples from the London, Associated Examination and Oxford Boards of the multiple choice, short answer and longer question. In each case a model answer is given with comments, but you should always try to do the questions yourself first and *then* check your answer with the model and comments. Do not ignore questions from boards different from your own; they may also be useful to you. The comments on the model answers try to stress the important points needed to obtain full marks and also to point out the parts of answers which, examiners report, are usually poorly answered.

It is important that you have a copy of the syllabus for your own board. This book is organized under subject headings mostly from the AEB syllabus, but it also covers the contents of the London, JMB, Oxford, Cambridge, and Oxford and Cambridge syllabuses. You should check your own syllabus against each section to see which parts you need to concentrate on. The units, letter symbols, signs and abbreviations used in this book are those used by the examiners themselves and generally follow those recommended in the ASE report *SI units, Signs, Symbols and Abbreviations*, revised in 1981.

This book cannot minimize the large amount of learning you have to do. Definitions, laws, practical details of experiments, derivations and applications of formulae have to be known and understood. The fact that all boards have either a paper or section of multiple choice questions or short answer questions means that a wide coverage of the syllabus is now examined and you cannot afford to leave parts out. This means there really is a great deal to learn. Do not leave this learning till the last minute, but try to plan your revision well in advance of the exam. You should also try to practise complete past papers to give you an opportunity to see whether you are working at the right speed and whether you can answer all the questions required and still have time in hand to check your work.

The chapter on exam technique is intended to help you when you face the paper so that you can tackle it intelligently. The examiners often comment on the number of students who do less well than they should because of poor exam technique – poorly presented work, questions not read carefully enough, poor diagrams without clear labelling, incorrect use of physics terms and absence of units. I hope this book will both help you to do yourself justice and give you confidence that you have prepared yourself properly as you go into the examination; you know and understand the subjects needed in your syllabus, you are ready for the sort of questions set and can answer them fully, clearly and in the way the examiners want.

Good luck in your physics O-level!

Section 2: Exam Technique

Even if you have learnt all your facts thoroughly it is possible that you will not do as well as you deserve because of poor exam technique. The London examiners spell out in their report the differences they see between Grade A and Grade C candidates:

The script submitted by a candidate awarded Grade A will generally be well set out and neat in appearance. The work will be logically presented and show an understanding and correct use of the language of Physics. Terms such as force, energy and pressure will be accurately used. The candidates will usually demonstrate that they understand the question and are aware of the significance of any detail given. The work of a candidate awarded a Grade C is typically less well set out and shows a lack of detail due to gaps in the candidate's knowledge. The point of the question may be missed and answers to some questions are vague and in non-Physics terms.

To try to help you, strategies for tackling the three different kinds of papers – multiple choice, short answer and long answer – will be considered separately.

Multiple Choice Papers

People often think these papers are easy. This is not so. As they contain a large number of questions they can cover almost all parts of the syllabus and so you cannot afford to miss out any parts. Furthermore, if you are to answer all the questions in the given time you need to work quickly, to recognize straight away what the question is asking, to have a good knowledge of basic definitions and formulae, and to be able to do simple calculations. It is important not to throw away marks by filling in the answer grid wrongly. Your physics teacher should show you a grid before your exam and you should be sure you know how to fill it in and how to change an answer should you need to. You will be given time at the beginning of the exam to read the instructions and check that you know exactly what to do.

There are several different kinds of multiple choice questions set in one paper. Examples of the most popular kinds are given below so that you can become used to dealing with them.

Multiple Choice

These questions have five alternative answers only *one* of which is correct. The other answers are known as distractors. You have to choose the correct answer.

Examination Question (LON)
A glass block of length 15 cm and refractive index 1·5 contains a small air bubble. Viewed from the side marked X the bubble appears *to be 6 cm from the side X. Viewed from the opposite side Y its distance from the side Y will* appear *to be:*

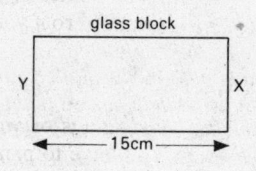

A *12 cm*   **B** *11 cm*   **C** *9 cm*   **D** *6 cm*   **E** *4 cm*

This question should immediately make you think of the basic formula

$$\text{refractive index} = \frac{\text{real depth}}{\text{apparent depth}}$$

As with many calculation problems it may help you to make rough notes and diagrams while solving this problem. Since only the answer grid is marked for this paper your rough work can be extremely rough. The comments on questions like this later in the book will help you to see what sort of rough work and thinking you need to do.

If bubble is x cm from X, $1\cdot 5 = \dfrac{x}{6}$

$x = 9$ cm

The bubble must be 6 cm (15 − 9) from Y,

so $1\cdot 5 = \dfrac{6}{y}$

$y = 4$ cm

So the answer is **E**. There is a lot of working out to do here (though the arithmetic is easy), and, unless you quickly recognize the correct formula to use, this question will take much longer than the one and a half minutes which London allows per question.

If you are reduced to guessing an answer, it is always worth guessing intelligently! With the question above, since you know that apparent depth is always less than the real depth, you know that the bubble must be more than 6 cm from X and so less than 9 cm from Y. The apparent depth from Y must therefore be less than 9 cm, and so distractors **A**, **B** and **C** can be discarded at once. You have therefore increased your guessing chances from 20 per cent to 50 per cent. It is always worth having a guess at a question if you cannot do it or run short of time, since both a wrong answer and no answer receive no marks. You always have a 20 per cent chance of being right with a random guess, which is better than a certain zero if you omit the question altogether.

Matching Pairs

Here a list of headings or words is given and two or three questions follow them. You have to pick the correct word from the list to answer the question. Remember you will not use all the words in the list and you may use one word more than once. These questions often test your knowledge of definitions and use of basic physics terms.

Examination Question (LON)
The following are associated with musical notes:
  A *amplitude* **B** *intensity* **C** *pitch* **D** *timbre (quality)* **E** *speed*
Which of the above
   (i) is determined by the fundamental frequency of the note?
   (ii) is constant for all sounds produced by an orchestra?
   (iii) can be used to distinguish between different musical instruments?
Answers: (i) **C** *(ii)* **E** *(iii)* **D**

When you tackle this kind of question you should read through the list of words, making a quick mental note of what you understand or know about each one. For example, you might think: 'amplitude – connected with the loudness of the note; pitch – connected with frequency and how high or low a note is; and so on. You are then fully prepared for the questions and should find them quick to answer.

Multiple Completion

Here each question has three responses, one or more of which are correct. When you have decided which is/are correct you have to follow the instructions given in the table shown below to find out whether to answer A, B, C, D or E. Do read these directions carefully. They will be given on each page on which this kind of question is given.

A	B	C	D	E
1, 2 and 3 correct	1, 2 only correct	2, 3 only correct	1 only correct	3 only correct

It is worth noting what is omitted here. You cannot have 2 only correct or 1, 3 only correct. If you find you think this should be so, think again!

Examination Question (AEB)
While a given mass of ice is changing from a solid state to the liquid state there is no change in its
           1 *mass*   2 *temperature*   3 *volume*

There is no comment about any loss of material so **1** is true. Your knowledge of change of state should tell you **2** is true. But your knowledge of the unusual behaviour of water on freezing tells you **3** must be wrong. So look in the table and you will see the correct answer is B.

These are the main types of questions you will find on your multiple choice paper. London also sets groups of questions of the multiple choice type on one practical situation. As long as you read the question carefully these should be straightforward.

When tackling the multiple choice paper you should work through it several times. On the first time through mark in any answers you know at once. On the second time through tackle more complicated calculations and think about questions you are dubious about. On the third run through tackle those about which you are really uncertain – if necessary making an intelligent guess but certainly putting in an answer for each question. Then check through your work if you still have time.

Short Answer Questions

Many boards that do not set multiple choice papers use a short answer paper instead. Often these questions are answered straight into an answer book, as is the case with Cambridge, London (from 1983 onwards), and Oxford and Cambridge. The amount of space left for an answer and the number of marks allocated for each part of the question will help you to decide how much detail you need to go into. You will find in the comments on such questions later in the book that this point is often stressed, and it is important that you do not waste time on irrelevant details. Clearly displayed calculations, proper statement of formulae, well-learnt definitions and clearly labelled diagrams will help you to score well in this paper. It is important to read the question carefully, to look out for the vital word – 'State', 'Describe', 'How', 'Why', 'Explain' or 'Calculate' – and to see that your answer has obeyed that instruction. Examiners work to a detailed marking scheme which indicates precisely how marks are to be allocated for each question. With short answer questions such marks are often for particular physics terms, so do try to use such words rather than vague, imprecise explanations. Again, this kind of paper covers a great deal of the syllabus and you need to have a wide understanding and knowledge of the facts. Two examples are given to show you how to tackle such questions.

Examination Question (LON)
A one-metre length of resistance wire, an ammeter and a 2·0 V cell are connected in series as shown in the figure below. (The ammeter and the cell have negligible resistance.)

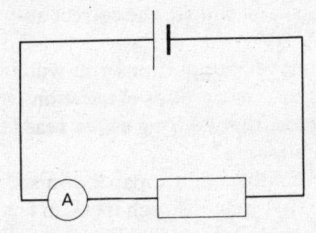

(a) The ammeter reads 0·50 A. Calculate the resistance of the resistance wire.
(b) The resistance wire is replaced by a one-metre length of wire of the same material but of twice the cross-sectional area. What is
  (i) the resistance of this wire,
  (ii) the new ammeter reading?
(c) A voltmeter is now connected across the resistance wire as shown in the figure below. Will the ammeter reading increase, decrease or remain the same? Give a reason for your answer. (6 marks)

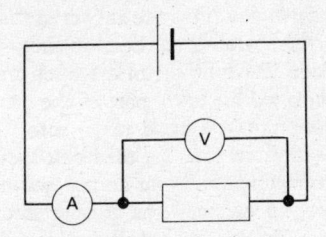

Answer
  This question is asking for several answers for only six marks, so you know it cannot be too complicated. You should always think of the formula you are going to use, quote it and then substitute the numbers from the question.

(a) $V = IR$
   $2\cdot 0(V) = 0\cdot 50(A) \times R(\Omega)$ (Don't forget that the ammeter measures *current*)
   $R = 4\Omega$

(b) (i) $R = \dfrac{\rho l}{A}$. Since the wire is of the same material, the resistivity ρ will be the same.

For the first wire: $4(\Omega) = \dfrac{\rho(\Omega m) \times 1(m)}{A(m^2)}$

For the second wire: $R(\Omega) = \dfrac{\rho(\Omega m) \times 1(m)}{2A(m^2)}$

$\therefore R = 2\Omega$

Alternatively, remember that $R \propto \dfrac{1}{A}$ for the same material and length, so that if the area is doubled the resistance must be halved.

(ii) $V = IR$
   $2\cdot 0(V) = I(A) \times 2(\Omega)$
   $I = 1A$

(c) The ammeter reading will go up slightly. The voltmeter has a high resistance. It is placed in parallel with the resistance wire, so the total resistance of the circuit decreases and the current therefore increases. Since they have not told you anything about the voltmeter, you must think about its resistance (which you know will be high) and the effect it will have on the circuit.

Examination Question (LON)
A person learning how to parachute jumps from a stationary tethered balloon in still air. Fig. (i) shows the person after he has jumped and Fig. (ii) shows him moving down after his parachute has opened. The arrows represent forces which act on the parachutist.
(a) Name the three forces A, B and C.
(b) What is the acceleration of the parachutist in Fig. (i)?
(c) What is the acceleration of the parachutist in Fig. (ii) if some time has elapsed since he jumped?
(7 marks)

Answer
(a) A – weight of parachutist
    B – weight of parachutist
    C – air resistance

Comment
Probably only one mark each so just state forces.

(b) Since parachutist is in free fall here, his acceleration is 10 m/s². (You were told in the question that he came 'from a stationary tethered balloon in still air', so you can assume he is in free fall.) The value for this acceleration is given on the front of the paper – a usual practice.

(c) The acceleration should be zero: as $B = C$ no unbalanced force acts on the parachutist and by *Newton's First Law* he will continue at a steady velocity. Since you are not given any numbers in this question you cannot calculate any acceleration, so you can guess that zero is the probable answer. If you have any knowledge at all about parachutes you would also expect this answer.

Longer Questions

These questions often appear on a paper where you have a choice of which question to answer. In order to choose sensibly, first read the paper through and mark those questions you feel are based on topics you understand best. Before you start answering a question do read it through again very carefully to be sure you know what it is asking. Answer first the question about which you feel most confident, and continue in this way until you have completed the right number. Remember to read the instructions at the beginning of the paper very carefully to make sure you choose the right number of questions from each section.

Some of these questions are highly structured. For an example, see pp. 32–6. You should tackle these as suggested for short answer questions. For the less structured questions it may be helpful to give yourself an answer plan as you read the question through. This will list the things you need to include in your answer and will probably include diagrams, some written work such as definitions, descriptions and explanations, and calculations, where you will usually need to state the relevant formula and substitute numbers from the question. Do remember that diagrams are very important in physics. Any question that includes the word 'describe' must have a clearly labelled diagram in the answer. Draw the diagram first, and then as you describe the apparatus and method of an experiment you can check that your words are consistent with the diagram. Such diagrams can save a lot of time.

Examiners point out that 'a common weakness with less able candidates is the reluctance to use Physics terms and these terms are specifically required by the Examiner if he is to award full marks'. Do take this to heart and see that your answer contains these terms – properly used, of course. Once again it is important to look for the key words in the question – 'Describe', 'Explain', 'Name', 'Account for', etc. – and to be sure that you have properly answered questions beginning 'How' and 'Why'.

Examiners also point out how weak candidates often are at giving experimental, practical detail, even when it is obvious that they have done the experiment themselves. AEB set a paper with questions relating to laboratory procedures and techniques specifically to test this, but all boards include questions of the type 'Describe an experiment to ...'. As well as diagrams, it is important to include the precautions you need to take: for example, keeping the key or switch closed for as short a time as possible in order to reduce heating losses in electrical experiments. Also, you should know where errors can occur in experiments: for example, ignoring the heat losses to the surroundings in heat experiments.

Do read your answer through when you think you have finished and check it against your answer plan to see that you have included everything necessary. At the end of the paper you should still have time to read your answers through again as a final check.

The Examination Boards

The addresses given below are those from which copies of syllabuses and past examination papers may be ordered. The abbreviations (AEB, etc.) are those used in the text to indicate the source of an exam question.

Associated Examining Board, (AEB)
Wellington House,
Aldershot, Hants GU11 1BQ

University of Cambridge Local Examination Syndicate, (CAM)
Syndicate Buildings, 17 Harvey Road,
Cambridge CB1 2EU

Joint Matriculation Board, (JMB)
(Agent) John Sherratt and Son Ltd,
78 Park Road,
Altrincham, Cheshire WA14 5QQ

University of London School Examinations Department, (LON)
66–72 Gower Street,
London WC1E 6EE

Northern Ireland Schools Examinations Council (NI)
Examinations Office,
Beechill House,
Beechill Road,
Belfast BT8 4RS

Oxford Delegacy of Local Examinations, (OXF)
Ewert Place,
Summertown,
Oxford OX2 7BZ

Oxford and Cambridge Schools Examination Board, (O & C)
10 Trumpington Street,
Cambridge CB2 1QB

Scottish Certificate of Education Examining Board, (SCO)
(Agent) Robert Gibson and Sons, Ltd,
17 Fitzroy Place,
Glasgow G3 7SF

Southern Universities Joint Board, (SUJB)
Cotham Road, Bristol BS6 6DD

Welsh Joint Education Committee, (WEL)
245 Western Avenue,
Cardiff CF5 2YX

Section 3: Mechanics and Properties of Matter

Mass, Length, Time, Density, Vectors

Fundamental quantities: **Mass** (unit: kilogram or gram); **time** (unit: second); **length** (unit: metre or centimetre).
Use of verniers and micrometers.
Measurements of **volume** (unit: m^3 or cm^3).
Measurement by displacement for irregular solids.

Density $= \dfrac{\text{Mass}}{\text{Volume}}$ (unit: kg/m^3 or g/cm^3)

Experimental determination of density.
Vectors: quantities that have magnitude *and* direction.
Scalars: quantities that have magnitude only.
Addition and subtraction of vectors (all calculations can be done using the **parallelogram of vectors** rule).
Components of vectors.

Multiple Choice Questions

Question 1 (AEB)
Which one of the following is not a vector quantity?

A Acceleration
B Displacement
C Force
D Speed
E Velocity

Answer: **D**
Since **D** and **E** stand for nearly the same idea it is likely to be one of them.

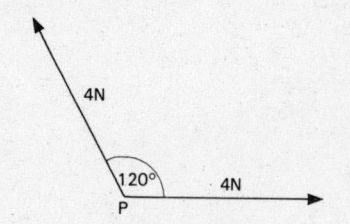

Question 2 (LON)
Two forces each of 4N act at a point P. The angle between the directions of the forces is 120°. The resultant of the two forces has a magnitude of

A 2 N
B 4 N
C 8 N
D 16 N
E none of the above

Answer: B

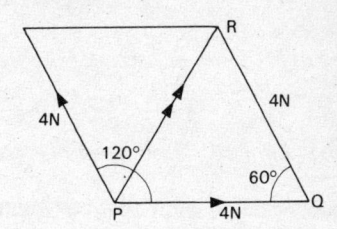

Really a geometry question!
Angle at Q must be 60° (angles of a parallelogram)
The triangle PQR is isosceles so angle QRP = QPR = 60°
∴ the triangle is equilateral so PR = 4 N

Question 3 (OXF)
A rectangular box has internal dimensions of 5 cm × 6 cm × 10 cm. The mass of the box is 50 g. It is completely filled with cubes of aluminium each of side 1 cm (take the density of aluminium to be 2·7 g/cm³). What is the total mass of the box and its contents?

A 131 g
B 212 g
C 760 g
D 810 g
E 860 g

Answer: E

Volume of one cube of aluminium
$$= 1 \text{ cm}^3$$

Mass = density × volume
mass of one cube of aluminium
$$= 2\cdot7 \text{ (g/cm}^3) \times 1 \text{ (cm}^3)$$
$$= 2\cdot7 \text{ g}$$

Volume of box
$$= 5 \text{ cm} \times 6 \text{ cm} \times 10 \text{ cm}$$
$$= 300 \text{ cm}^3$$
∴ no. of cubes = 300
mass of cubes
$$= 300 \times 2\cdot7 \text{ g}$$
$$= 810 \text{ g}$$

Mass of box + contents
$$= 810 \text{ g} + 50 \text{ g}$$
$$= 860 \text{ g}$$

Longer Questions

Question 1 (LON)
(a) What do you understand by the resultant of two forces acting at a point?
(2 marks)

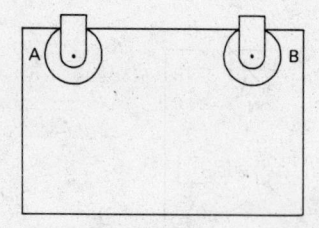

(b) The diagram shows two pulleys A and B, clamped to a vertical board. Describe how, using this apparatus and some standard masses, it can be shown that under certain conditions forces of 3 N and 4 N can be kept in equilibrium by a 5 N force.
What is the relationship between the 5 N force and the resultant of the 3 N and 4 N forces? (You may assume the gravitational force acting on a 1 kg mass is 10 N.) *(8 marks)*
(c) The diagram below represents a boat being towed along a canal by a person walking along the bank. The tow rope is horizontal and makes an angle of 30° with the bank; the tension in the rope is 200 N.

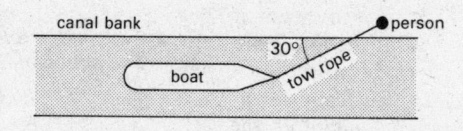

(i) What is the effective force which pulls the boat forward?
(ii) What is the effective force which pulls the boat sideways towards the bank?
(iii) What is the resultant horizontal force acting on the boat if it is moving along the canal at a constant velocity? *(7 marks)*
It is sometimes recommended, when towing a boat along a canal, that the length of the rope should be as long as possible. Suggest the reason for this and justify your answer using your knowledge of physics.
(3 marks)

Answer

(a) When two **forces** are acting together at a point it is always possible to find a single force which will have the same effect as these forces. This single force is called the **resultant force**.

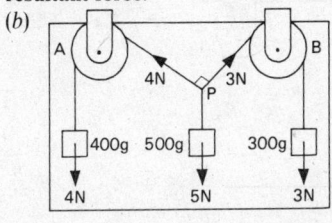

(b)

```
   A ⊙         ⊙ B
       4N \ / 3N
           P
    ┌──┐ ┌──┐   ┌──┐
    │400g│500g│   │300g│
    └──┘ └──┘   └──┘
     4N    5N     3N
```

10 N is force on 1 kg mass
∴ 5 N is force on 500 g mass,
   4 N is force on 400 g mass,
   3 N is force on 300 g mass.

The standard masses are tied to string or cotton and arranged as shown in the diagram above. When the system is in equilibrium and has been checked for free movement, it will settle such that the forces are as shown in the diagram.
The 5 N force acts vertically downwards, while the resultant of the 3 N and 4 N force acts vertically upwards and exactly balances it.

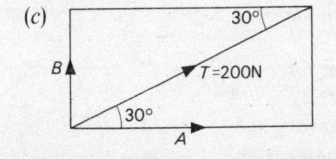

(c)
```
              30°
    B ◄──────T=200N
       \30°
         A ──►
```

Comment

Give answer in words.
Remember: the resultant can replace the two original forces, so it must have exactly the same effect as they do.

Obviously, you are going to add things to their apparatus, so draw it again and put in your choice of standard masses. Remember: 'Describe' should make you think of a diagram at once.

Make the angle at P look like a right angle (3, 4, 5 triangle), and make $\dfrac{\text{AP}}{\text{BP}}$ look roughly like $\tfrac{4}{3}$, but do not waste time drawing it to scale. Mark on the diagram the direction and magnitude of the forces.
  Give experimental details as well (examiners always feel people skimp on these). Remember: masses take time to settle. Since forces are balanced one must be up and one down.

One force given in question and you are asked for two 'effective forces', so this should make you think of *components*.
A diagram is always a help in explaining components and can be used later in the question if you label the components with letters.

T can be considered as being made up of two forces *A* and *B* at right angles to each other as shown in the diagram.

(i) Force pulling boat forward
$$= A$$
$$= 200 \cos 30° \text{ N}$$
$$= 173 \cdot 2 \text{ N}$$

(ii) Force pulling boat to bank
$$= B$$
$$= 200 \sin 30° \text{ N}$$
$$= 100 \text{ N}$$

(iii) Since the boat moves with constant velocity no unbalanced force acts on it.
∴ The resultant horizontal force acting on the boat is zero.

N.B. constant velocity: this must have some importance or they would not mention it (examiners said in report that only 1 mark was given for this section and it was hardly ever awarded!).

The longer the tow rope the smaller it is possible to make the angle between the rope and the bank. This makes component *A* larger (the useful force) and component *B* smaller.

Think about this practically. Picture yourself with a long rope and a short rope, and you should be able to see that it is the angle between rope and bank which changes.

Question 2 (OXF)
A bath 2 m long and 0·6 m wide is filled with water at a steady rate from a tap to a depth of 0·4 m in 8 minutes. (Take the density of water to be 1000 kg/m³.)
(a) What volume of water is used? (2 marks)
(b) What volume of water comes from the tap every second? (2 marks)
(c) What is the total mass of water used? (2 marks)
(d) If the water travels along a pipe to the tap at 10 m/s what is the cross-sectional area of this pipe? (2 marks)
(e) If the bath were filled to the same depth with brine, of density 1200 kg/m³, what mass of brine would be needed? (2 marks)

Answer
(a) Volume = length × width
 × depth

Comment
Quote formula used.

Mechanics and Properties of Matter 23

$V = 2\text{ m} \times 0.6\text{ m}$
$\phantom{V = 2\text{ m}} \times 0.4\text{ m}$
$= 0.48\text{ m}^3$

Careful about units of volume.

(b) Volume in 8 minutes = 0.48 m^3
volume in 1 second
$$= \frac{0.48}{8 \times 60}\text{ m}^3/\text{s}$$
$$= 0.001\text{ m}^3/\text{s}$$

This kind of question often uses results found in one section in the next one. N.B. 60 seconds in a minute. Be careful over more complicated units here.

(c) Density = $\dfrac{\text{mass}}{\text{volume}}$

∴ mass = volume × density
$= 0.48\text{ m}^3$
$ \times 1000\text{ kg/m}^3$
$= 480\text{ kg}$

Quote formula.

Use answer from (a) not (b) as time is not involved here.

Units!

(d) Volume/s of water = $0.0001/\text{m}^3/\text{s}$
Volume/s = length/s
$\phantom{\text{Volume/s} = }\times$ area of cross-section
$0.001\text{ m}^3/\text{s} = 10\text{ m/s} \times A$
$A = 0.0001\text{ m}^2$

Here time comes in again.
$v = 10\text{ m/s}$
Volume = length × area
Vol./s. = (length × area)/s.
Vol./s. = length/s. × area
Units!

(e) Volume of liquid is unchanged.
Mass = volume × density
$= 0.48\text{ m}^3 \times 1200\text{ kg/m}^3$
$= 576\text{ kg}$

Important to show you know this, so say it.

Question 3
(a)

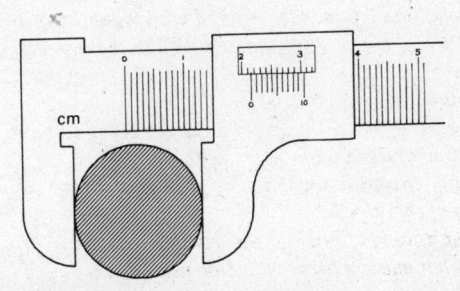

What is the reading on the vernier calipers shown above?
(b) What is the difference between a vector and a scalar quantity? Give one example of a vector and one example of a scalar quantity.

Answer
(a) 2·15 cm

Comment
(1) Look at the 0 mark on vernier scale; which mark has it just passed? Here, 2·1.

(2) See which line on vernier scale exactly meets a line on the main scale. Here the 5 mark, so reading is 2·15.

(3) Remember units.

(b) A *vector* quantity has magnitude *and* direction.
A *scalar* quantity has magnitude only.
A *vector* quantity is weight.
A *scalar* quantity is mass.

You need to know these definitions, and you should always learn one example of each as you are often asked for them.

Question 4
How would you measure the density of an irregular solid such as a glass stopper? If the mass of the glass stopper is 65 g and the volume is 25 cm³, what is its density? (*10 marks*)

Answer

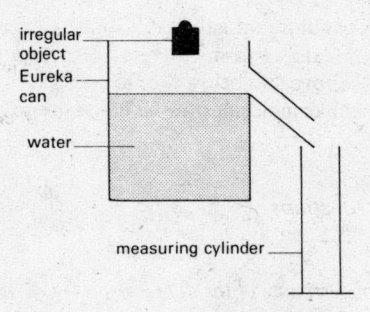

[Diagram showing irregular object, Eureka can, water, and measuring cylinder]

$$\text{Density} = \frac{\text{mass}}{\text{volume}}$$

The mass is measured on a beam balance. The volume is found by

Comment
Give formula for density so it is clear what you need to measure.

'Describe': use a well-labelled diagram to help here. Since it is an lowering the object gently into the Eureka can, which is filled to the edge of its spout. The amount of water displaced is measured in the measuring cylinder. This is equal to the volume of the object. The procedure should be repeated two or three times, and the average volume found. The density can then be obtained by dividing the mass (g) by the volume (cm^3) to give a density in g/cm^3.

irregular object you should think of a displacement method at once.

$$\text{Density} = \frac{\text{mass}}{\text{volume}}$$
$$= \frac{65 \text{ (g)}}{25 \text{ (cm}^3\text{)}}$$
$$= 2 \cdot 6 \text{ g/cm}^3$$

State formula and substitute numbers. Be careful of units.

Particulate Nature of Matter

Distinction between solids, liquids and gases in terms of molecular motion and energies.
Brownian motion in liquids and gases (this topic will be studied in detail in Section 4 under 'Heat as a form of energy. Kinetic energy', pp. 77–80)
Behaviour of solids above and below the elastic unit.
Adhesive (between unlike molecules) and **cohesive** (between like molecules) forces.

Multiple Choice Questions

Question 1 (LON)
What is a reasonable estimate of the diameter of a molecule?

A 10^{-1} mm
B 10^{-3} mm
C 10^{-6} mm
D 10^{-10} mm
E 10^{-15} mm

Answer: C
You should try to have an idea of the size of physical quantities like this, otherwise there is nothing to guide you and you will have to guess.

Question 2 (OXF)
An air-filled gas jar contains a small capsule of bromine at the bottom. The capsule is broken and the jar immediately sealed. Which one of the following describes what would then be seen?

A *A layer of brown bromine gas forms at the bottom of the jar and remains there since bromine is more dense than air.*
B *The bromine gas rises to form a brown layer at the top of the jar since bromine is less dense than air.*
C *The brown colour of the bromine gas slowly disappears as the bromine is absorbed by the air.*
D *The brown bromine gas rises up the centre of the jar and down the sides as a convection current.*
E *The brown bromine gas slowly rises and eventually fills the jar as the bromine molecules intermingle with the air molecules.*

Answer: E

A and **B** are unlikely, as you cannot be expected to know the density of bromine.

C sounds chemically unlikely.

Question 3 (LON)
A piece of cotton thread is attached to the midpoints of opposite sides of a rectangular wire frame. The frame is dipped in soap solution and a soap film forms across the frame with the thread lying loosely in the film as shown below.

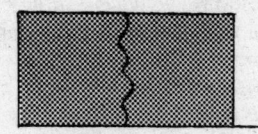

The part of the film to the left of the thread is broken. Which diagram below shows the shape of the film now?

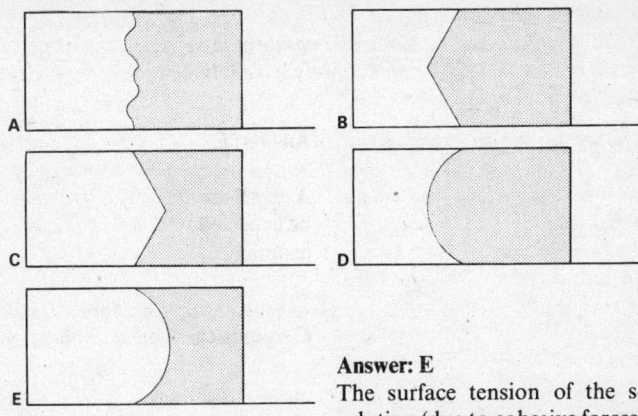

Answer: E
The surface tension of the soap solution (due to cohesive forces between the soap molecules) pulls on the cotton and tries to make the surface area as small as possible; the cotton therefore forms a circular arc as in **E**, since the force is at 90° to the surface.

Longer questions

Question 1 (A E B part question)
A student in estimating the size of an oil molecule formed a small oil drop, of diameter d mm, on a loop of wire. The student then placed the oil drop gently on still water and measured the diameter D mm of the resulting oil film. Assuming the oil film is one molecule thick, show how the student could estimate the size of the oil molecule.

Answer
Volume of oil in drop

$$= \frac{4}{3}\pi\left(\frac{d}{2}\right)^3 \text{ mm}^3$$

The spherical drop spread out forms a cylinder one molecule thick.

Comment
Don't forget the formula for volume of a sphere is usually in terms of radius, and that you are interested in diameter (twice radius).

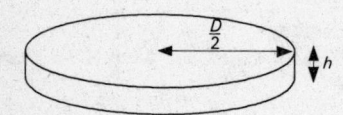

Let the length of the molecule be h mm.

Vol. of spread oil $= \pi\left(\dfrac{D}{2}\right)^2 h$ mm^3

$\dfrac{4}{3}\pi\left(\dfrac{d}{2}\right)^2 = \pi\left(\dfrac{D}{2}\right)^2 h$

Whence h.

A diagram will often help you think what is happening.

Now a cylinder not a sphere.

As long as you get a formula which will give you h there is no need to calculate it. 'Whence' is a very useful word.

Question 2 (LON)
Explain the following, bringing in where possible the behaviour of molecules.

(a) When gamboge (or graphite) particles suspended in water are observed through a microscope, they are seen to move in a random way. (4 marks)

(b) A steel needle placed carefully on the surface of water does not sink. When a small drop of detergent is placed on the water the needle moves rapidly away from it, and sinks when more detergent is added. (You may assume that detergent does not affect the density of water.) (6 marks)

(c) When water is poured carefully on to some copper(II) sulphate solution in a beaker there is a clear demarcation line between the liquids, but after two or three days the solution is a uniform blue. (5 marks)

(d) The apparatus is set up as shown in the diagram (below). The level of the liquid in A is observed to rise before coming to rest, but that in B is observed to fall until it is level with the surface of the water in the trough. (5 marks)

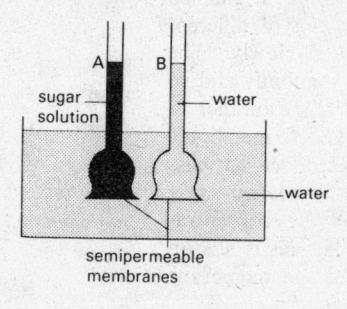

Answer
(a) Molecules are considered to be in constant motion, their energy depending on their temperature and state (solid, liquid or gas). The water molecules (too small to be seen) collide with the gamboge particles and make them seem to move in a random way as they themselves do.

(b) The surface tension of the water surface holds the needle up as shown in the diagram. When the detergent is added it settles in the surface of the liquid since it has one **hydrophilic** and one **hydrophobic** end. It therefore disturbs the molecular arrangement at the surface of the water and reduces the surface tension, so the needle first moves away from the detergent and then sinks.

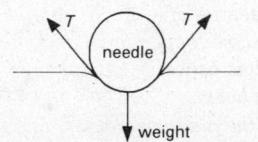

(c) Liquid molecules move slowly relative to those of a gas, so **diffusion**, the mixing of different substances, occurs slowly. The molecules move randomly and so gradually mix with one another.

(d) The semipermeable membrane allows water molecules to pass through it but not the larger sugar molecules. Since the concentration of water molecules is less on the sugar side of the membrane

Comment
Brownian motion in a liquid.

Floating needle, so think of surface tension.

Hydrophilic – water loving.
Hydrophobic – water hating.

A diagram, no matter how rough, will help your explanation.
T is surface tension force.

An important point to recognize and state is that this is *diffusion*.

You should recognize this common textbook diagram, and the words 'semipermeable membrane' should immediately make you think of *osmosis*.

(because of the space the sugar molecules take up), water will pass into the sugar solution and the level in A will rise. This is **osmosis**. In B the water can pass through the membrane and so the water level will fall until it is level with the surface of the water in the trough.

Remember to put your explanation in terms of molecules as the question asks.

Motion in a Straight Line

Velocity = rate of change of displacement with time. Unit: m/s or cm/s.
Acceleration = rate of change of velocity with time. Unit: m/s^2 or cm/s^2.
Displacement–time graphs and velocity–time graphs.
Equations of motion for constant acceleration in a straight line; the usual symbols are: initial velocity, u; final velocity, v; time, t; acceleration, a; displacement, s. The equations are: $v = u + at$; $s = ut + \frac{1}{2}at^2$; $v^2 - u^2 = 2as$; $s = \frac{1}{2}(v + u)t$.

Motion of bodies under **gravity** and determination of acceleration due to gravity (g).

Multiple Choice Questions

Question 1(A E B)
An object changes its speed uniformly from 60 m/s to 40 m/s in 5 s. Its acceleration in m/s^2 is

A -4
B -10
C -20
D -50
E -100

Answer: A
Use definition of *acceleration*:

$$a = \frac{\text{change in velocity}}{\text{time}}$$

$$= \frac{v - u}{t} = \frac{40 - 60}{5}$$

$$= -4 \text{ m/s}^2$$

Mechanics and Properties of Matter 31

Question 2 (OXF)

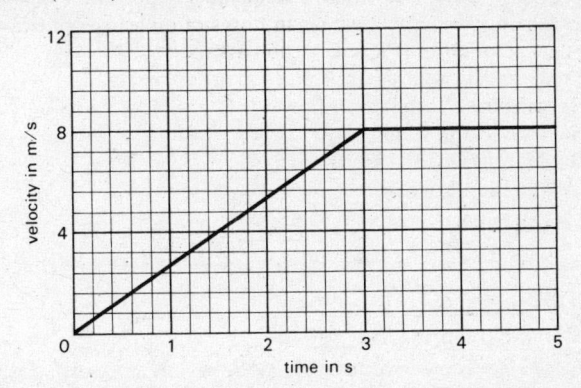

The graph represents the velocity of a moving trolley plotted against the time for which it is in motion. How far will the trolley have travelled after 5 seconds?

A *7 m*
B *20 m*
C *28 m*
D *40 m*
E *52 m*

Answer: C
Distance travelled = area under graph
Divide area up into triangle and rectangle.
Area △ = $\frac{1}{2}$ base × height
       = $\frac{1}{2}$ × 3 × 8 = 12 m
Area ☐ = base × height = 2 × 8
       = 16 m

∴ total distance = 28 m

Question 3 (LON)

A stone is dropped from rest from the top of a tall building. The fraction $\left(\dfrac{\text{distance travelled in the first 4 seconds}}{\text{distance travelled in the first 2 seconds}}\right)$ is approximately

A $\dfrac{1}{4}$

B $\dfrac{1}{2}$

Answer: D
Falling under gravity, so $a = g$.
(1) $u = 0$ $s_1 = ?$ $a = g$ $t = 4$
(2) $u = 0$ $s_2 = ?$ $a = g$ $t = 2$

C $\dfrac{2}{1}$

D $\dfrac{4}{1}$

E $\dfrac{16}{1}$

$s = ut + \tfrac{1}{2}at^2$
$s_1 = \tfrac{1}{2}g16 = 8g$
$s_2 = \tfrac{1}{2}g4 = 2g$

$\therefore \dfrac{s_1}{s_2} = \dfrac{4}{1}$

Question 4 (AEB)

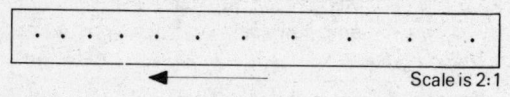

Scale is 2:1

The diagram shows a series of dots which were printed at equal time intervals on a tape moving in the direction shown. The tape moved with

A a constant velocity followed by a constant acceleration
B a constant velocity followed by a constant retardation
C a constant acceleration throughout
D a constant retardation throughout
E a constant velocity with a sudden increase to a higher constant velocity

Answer: A
Place your ruler against the tape, and you will see that the left-hand dots are equally spaced and that they then grow steadily further apart.

Longer Questions

Question 1 (OXF)
(a) Complete the statements:
A steady __(1)__ is required to make a trolley accelerate uniformly. If the trolley starts from rest, its velocity at a given moment can be calculated by multiplying the __(2)__ by the __(3)__ . This motion can be represented by a sloping straight line on a graph of the __(4)__ against the __(5)__ .
(5 marks)
(b) A thin strip of paper tape pulled by a trolley has a dot made on it every $\tfrac{1}{50}$ second by a stationary vibrator (ticker-tape timer). The diagram shows a length of this tape with dots made as the trolley rolls down a gentle slope.

Scale is 2:1

(i) What sort of motion does the tape represent? (1 mark)
(ii) How far has the trolley moved between the first and the eleventh dots? (2 marks)
(iii) What is the time interval between the first and the eleventh dots? (1 mark)
(iv) What value does this give for the trolley's speed? (2 marks)
(v) Draw a tape to show how the tape would look if the speed of the trolley were twice as fast. (2 marks)

(c) The trolley is replaced at the top of the track and pulled down it by a constant force. The tape is then cut into lengths of five dots each. The lengths are glued to paper as shown below to produce a block graph.

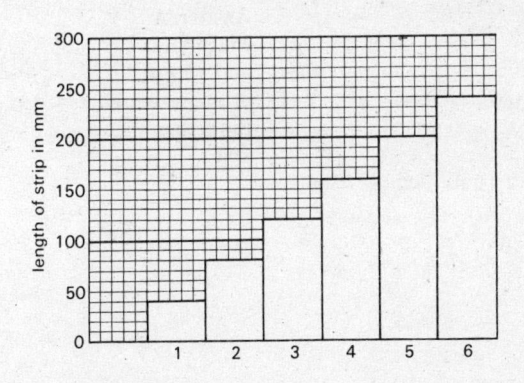

(i) How long does it take for each strip to receive five dots? (1 mark)
(ii) How fast did the trolley travel for:

strip 1?   strip 6? (2 marks)

(iii) What was the average velocity of the trolley during the time taken for:

strip 1?   strip 6? (3 marks)

(iv) What was the increase in velocity between the times for strip 1 and strip 6? (2 marks)
(v) What was the acceleration of the trolley? (2 marks)

(d) A graph of the speed of a boy on a bicycle against time is shown below.

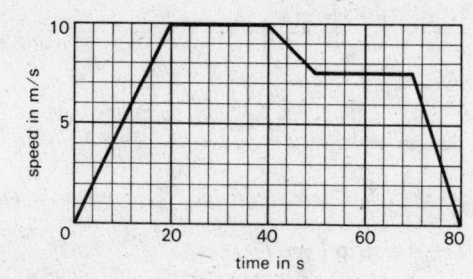

(i) Describe the journey in terms of the motion of the boy (without making any calculations). *(4 marks)*
(ii) How far did he travel during the first 40 seconds? *(3 marks)*

Answer	Comment
(a) (1) force (2) acceleration (3) time (4) velocity (5) time	Obviously one mark per word – so guess if you don't know. (2) and (3) can be either way round
(b) (i) uniform velocity (ii) 12 cm	Dots are equally spaced. Measure it!
(iii) Time between dots = $\frac{1}{50}$ s ∴ time between first and eleventh dot = $\frac{10}{50}$ s = 0.2 s	Count time intervals *not* dots.
(iv) Speed = $\frac{\text{distance}}{\text{time}}$ = $\frac{12 \text{ (cm)}}{0 \cdot 2 \text{ (s)}}$ = 60 cm/s	Quote formula used. N.B. units.
(v)	Scale is 2:1 Since the trolley is going faster, the dots will be more spread out. For twice the speed, the distance between the dots must be doubled.

(c) (i) Time between dots is $\frac{1}{50}$ s

∴ time for five dots $= 5 \times \frac{1}{50}$ s

$= \frac{1}{10}$ s

(ii) From the graph: Read straight off graph.

distance travelled for strip 1 = 40 mm

distance travelled for strip 6 = 240 mm

(iii) Velocity $= \dfrac{\text{distance}}{\text{time}}$

3 marks: probably one for each answer and one for quoting the formula.

For strip 1: average velocity

$= \dfrac{40 \text{ (mm)}}{1/10 \text{ (s)}}$

$= 400$ mm/s

For strip 6: average velocity

$= \dfrac{240 \text{ (mm)}}{1/10 \text{ (s)}}$

$= 2400$ mm/s

(iv) Increase in velocity
$= 2400 - 400$ mm/s
$= 2000$ mm/s
$= 2$ m/s

(v) Acceleration   Quote formula.

$= \dfrac{\text{change in velocity}}{\text{time}}$

$= \dfrac{2 \text{ (m/s)}}{\text{time between strip 1 and strip 6}}$

Each strip lasts 0·1 s

∴ time between strip 1 and strip 6
$= 0.5$ s

Think practically how you would do the experiment, and so how long there is between strip 1 and strip 6.

∴ acceleration = $\dfrac{2 \text{ (m/s)}}{0.5 \text{ (s)}}$

or $\dfrac{2000 \text{ (mm/s)}}{0.5 \text{ (s)}}$

= 4 m/s/s
or 4000 mm/s/s

(d) (i) The boy starts from rest and accelerates uniformly for 20 s. He then cycles at a steady velocity of 10 m/s for 20 s, decelerates uniformly for 10 s, stays at his new lower speed of 7·5 m/s for 20 s and then decelerates uniformly to rest in 20 s.

(ii) Distance travelled = area under the graph

$D = (\tfrac{1}{2} \times 20 \times 10) + (20 \times 10)$ m
= 100 + 200 m
= 300 m

Start at the beginning of the graph and describe his motion in terms of *accelerations, decelerations* and *steady speeds*. Put in your answer anything easily read from the graph (like times involved), but don't bother to work out accelerations, etc.

Divide the area into a suitable triangle and rectangle and add areas together.

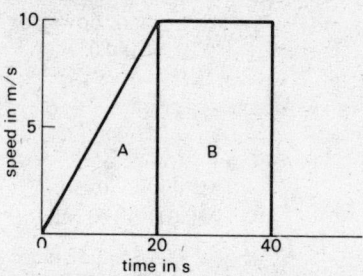

Question 2 (LON part question)

The speed of a train which is hauled by a locomotive varies as shown below as it travels between two stations along a straight horizontal track.

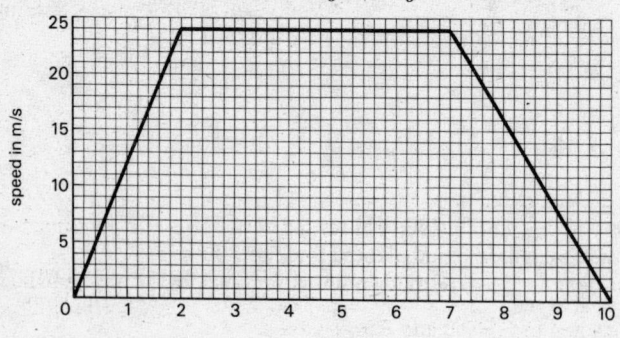

Mechanics and Properties of Matter 37

Use the graph to determine
(a) the maximum speed of the train,
(b) the acceleration in m/s² of the train during the first two minutes of the journey,
(c) the time taken during which the train is slowing down,
(d) the total distance, in metres, between the two stations along the line,
(e) the average speed in m/s of the train. (*14 marks*)

Answer
(a) The maximum speed is 24 m/s.
(b) Acceleration
$$= \frac{\text{change in velocity}}{\text{time}}$$
$$= \frac{24 \text{ (m/s)} - 0 \text{ (m/s)}}{120 \text{ (s)}}$$
$$= 0.2 \text{ m/s}^2$$
(c) The train is slowing down for 3 minutes (or 180 seconds).
(d) Total distance
 = Area under graph
 = ½ × 120 (s) × 24 (m/s)
  + 24 (m/s) × 300 (s)
  + ½ × 180 (s) × 24 (m/s)
 = 1440 + 7200 + 2160 (m)
 = 10 800 m
(e) Average speed = $\frac{\text{total distance}}{\text{total time}}$

Comment
Read it straight off the graph.

Remember to convert time into seconds.

Think of the graph as two triangles and one rectangle:

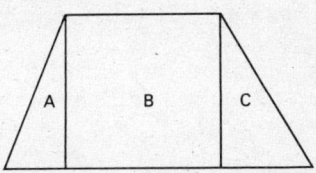

Area of △ = ½ (base × height)
Area of □ = base × height
Don't forget to convert time into seconds.

Laws of Motion

Newton's laws of motion:
(1) every body stays in a state of rest or of uniform velocity (magnitude *and* direction) unless an unbalanced force acts on it,
(2) the rate of change of momentum is proportional to the unbalanced force, leading to $F = ma$ and $F = \frac{mv - mu}{t}$,

(3) to every action there is an equal and opposite reaction.

Momentum = $m \times v$

Conservation of momentum.

Weight and **friction.**

Multiple Choice Questions

Question 1 (LON multiple completion)
A constant force F pulls a body along a rough horizontal surface.

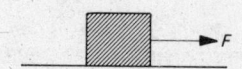

If no acceleration is produced it may be deduced that

1 *force F is equal to the weight of the body*
2 *frictional force is constant*
3 *frictional force is opposite in direction to force F*

Answer: 2 and 3
Weight always acts vertically downwards, so it is at right angles to *F* and will not be affected by it. Then think of *Newton's first law*.

Question 2 (OXF)
The speed of a trolley of mass 2 kg increased from 1 m/s to 5 m/s in a time of 2 s when acted upon by a steady force in the direction of its motion. What is the magnitude of the force?

A *2 N*
B *4 N*
C *5 N*
D *8 N*
E *10 N*

Answer: B

$$F = ma = \frac{m(v - u)}{t}$$
$$= \frac{2 \times (5 - 1)}{2} = 4 \text{ N}$$

Question 3 (AEB)
Five identical stationary trucks are already joined together when a sixth identical truck (moving at 2 m/s) couples with them so that they all move together. Their speed in m/s immediately after the coupling is

A $\dfrac{1}{3}$

B $\dfrac{2}{5}$

C $\sqrt{\dfrac{2}{3}}$

D $\dfrac{5}{6}$

E $1\dfrac{2}{3}$

Answer: A
Conservation of momentum:

momentum before collision = momentum after collision

$(m \times 2) + (5m \times 0) = (6m \times v)$

$$v = \dfrac{1}{3}$$

Question 4 (AEB)

A mass of 1 kg is secured to the hook of a spring balance calibrated on the Earth. The spring balance reading is first observed when it is freely suspended at rest just above the Earth's surface, secondly, inside a spaceship orbiting round the Earth and, finally, at rest on the Moon's surface. If the acceleration due to free fall on the Earth is 10 m/s^2 and the acceleration due to free fall on the Moon is 1·6 m/s^2, the spring balance readings, in N, would be

	Above the Earth's surface	Inside a spaceship	On the Moon
A	1·0	0	0·16
B	1·0	0·84	0·16
C	10·0	0	1·6
D	10·0	0·84	0·16
E	10·0	11·6	1·6

Answer: C
Remember:
$$W = mg$$
On Earth:
$$mg = 1 \text{ (kg)} \times 10 \text{ (m/s}^2)$$
$$= 10 \text{ N}$$
On Moon:
$$mg = 1 \text{ (kg)} \times 1 \cdot 6 \text{ (m/s}^2)$$
$$= 1 \cdot 6 \text{ N}$$
On spaceship:
$$g = 0$$
$$\therefore mg = 0$$

Longer Questions

Question 1 (LON)

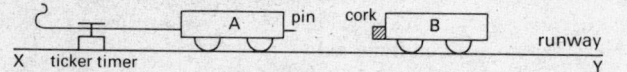

The diagram illustrates an experiment with trolleys and a ticker timer. Trolley A is given a slight push and collides with trolley B. The pin penetrates the cork so that both trolleys stick together and move as one. The tape obtained is shown, full size, alongside a millimetre grid below. The time interval between each dot is 0·02 s.

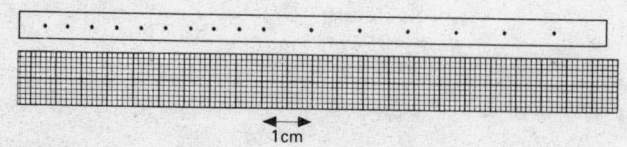

(a) Before carrying out the experiment, it is usual to make an adjustment which results in end X of the runway being slightly higher than end Y.

(i) What is the purpose of this adjustment and why is it necessary?
(ii) Has the adjustment been carried out in this case? Give a reason for your answer. *(5 marks)*

(b) Using the tape, determine:

(i) the average speed, in cm/s, of trolley A before the collision,
(ii) the time which has elapsed before the collision takes place,
(iii) the average speed, in cm/s, of the two trolleys A and B after the collision. *(7 marks)*

(c) A textbook states: 'When two bodies collide the total momentum is conserved but the total kinetic energy is not conserved.'

(i) Using the results given below, which were obtained in a further experiment, test the truth or otherwise of both parts of the above statement.

Mass of trolley A = 0·8 kg
Mass of trolley B = 2·4 kg
Velocity of trolley A before collision = 40 cm/s
Velocity of trolley B before collision = 0 cm/s
Velocity of trolleys A and B after collision = 10 cm/s *(6 marks)*

(ii) If either or both of the quantities are not conserved suggest a reason or reasons for the non-conservation. *(2 marks)*

Answer
(a) (i) The end of the runway is adjusted so that A will move with constant velocity. The component of its weight along the track should then exactly balance the frictional force between the trolley and the runway.

(ii) The adjustment has been carried out in this case because the distance between the dots is constant at the start of the tape.

(b)(i) Distance between dots at start
$= 0.9$ cm
Time between dots $= 0.02$ s

$$\text{Speed} = \frac{\text{distance}}{\text{time}}$$

$$= \frac{0.9}{0.02} \text{ cm/s}$$

$$= 45 \text{ cm/s}$$

(ii) The collision occurs when the dot spacing changes. There are seven intervals between the first dot and the collision
$\therefore$ time interval $= 7 \times 0.02$
$= 0.14$ s

(iii) After collision, the distance between dots $= 0.3$ cm

$$\text{Speed} = \frac{\text{distance}}{\text{time}}$$

$$= \frac{0.3}{0.02} \text{ cm/s}$$

$$= 15 \text{ cm/s}$$

(c) (i) **Momentum = mass × velocity**
Before collision:
momentum $= 0.8(\text{kg}) \times 40(\text{cm/s})$
$+ 2.4(\text{kg}) \times 0(\text{cm/s})$
$= 32$ kg cm/s

Comment
Think about when you did the experiment.

Make sure your answer to (ii) corresponds to (i).

Use their scale to measure.

Show that you know where the collision occurs.

Define *momentum* (p. 38).

After collision, trolleys stick together:
momentum = 3·2(kg) × 10 (cm/s)
= 32 kg cm/s
∴ momentum is conserved.

Consider the situation before and after the collision.

Kinetic energy = $\frac{1}{2}mv^2$

Define *kinetic energy* (p. 52).

Before collision:
kinetic energy = $\frac{1}{2}$ × 0·8 (kg) × (40 cm/s)^2 + $\frac{1}{2}$ × 2·4 (kg) × (0 cm/s)^2
= 640 kg cm^2/s^2

After collision:

kinetic energy = $\frac{1}{2}$ × 3·2 (kg) × (10 cm/s)^2
= 160 kg cm^2/s^2

∴ kinetic energy is not conserved.

(ii) The kinetic energy is not conserved since energy is lost during the collision. Some work needs to be done in driving the pin into the cork.

Only 2 marks, but think of the obvious reason why energy is lost.

Question 2
Why does a gun recoil when it is fired?

Answer
In an enclosed system the total momentum is conserved. When a gun is fired the bullet leaves the gun with a forward velocity. Momentum is a *vector* quantity, so the gun must recoil:
(mass of bullet × velocity of bullet) + (mass of gun × velocity of gun)
= 0
as the gun and bullet were stationary to begin with.

Comment
State law of *conservation of momentum* and then give formula for the firing situation.

Question 3 (OXF)

A trolley runs freely down a small angled slope at constant speed. It pulls a length of ticker tape through a timer which marks a dot every $\frac{1}{50}$ s. On a second run the trolley is given a steady pull down the slope.

(a) Draw a diagram of all the forces acting on the trolley on the first run, and explain why the speed is constant. *(4 marks, 2 marks)*

(b) Explain how a steady pull could be provided for the second run and describe a way of providing a steady pull of twice the size.
(2 marks, 2 marks)

(c) Describe how to use the apparatus to measure the acceleration of the trolley for a given force, and hence to show that acceleration is proportional to force. *(4 marks, 2 marks)*

(d) Describe how to use the apparatus to investigate the variation between acceleration and mass of the trolley for a constant force. Sketch a suitable graph which could be used to display the results and explain what you would expect to find. *(2 marks, 2 marks)*

Answer
(a)

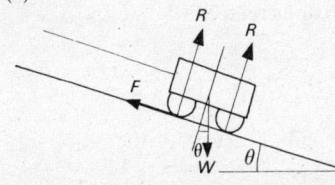

Comment

Remember that W here has *components* along and perpendicular to the slope.

Resolving along the slope, $W \sin \theta = F$ if there is no acceleration (**Newton's first law**). So if θ is adjusted for this to be true there will be a constant velocity.

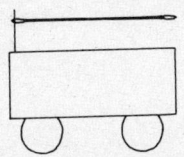

(b) An elastic cord is attached to a stick at the end of the trolley, which is pulled so that it is always level with the front of the trolley. For twice the pull, a second elastic cord

Think back to when you did this practical, and describe your set-up.

just like the first is put on the stick and pulled to the same distance.

(c) For each force, pull the trolley down the slope and study the ticker tape. Cut the tape into five space intervals (representing 0·1 s) and paste onto graph.

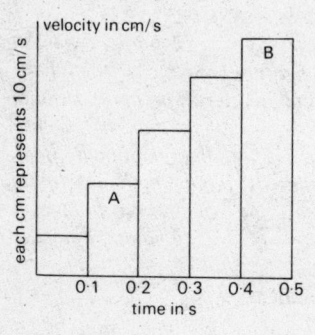

A diagram of the results will help you to explain what you are doing.

Then calculate:

$$\text{acceleration} = \frac{v_B - v_A}{\text{time}_B - \text{time}_A}$$

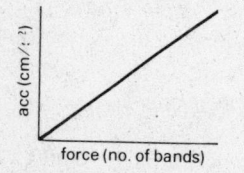

Again, a sketch of the graph you expect will help to make your answer clear.

For each force calculate the acceleration, plot a graph of acceleration versus force, and a straight line passing through the origin should be obtained showing that acceleration is proportional to force.

Mechanics and Properties of Matter 45

(d) One force is used constantly in this experiment, but the number of trolleys is varied. The acceleration is calculated as above for each situation, and a graph of $\dfrac{1}{\text{acceleration}}$ against mass is plotted (either the trolleys can be weighed or taken as 1 m, 2 m, 3 m, etc.).

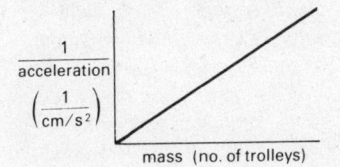

You know $F = ma$, so if F is constant $\dfrac{1}{a} \propto m$.

Only 4 marks in all, so don't go into a lot of detail.

Static Systems

This section has various different names or comes under different headings for the various boards. Look at the list of contents and you will probably find them under the first paragraph or two of your syllabus: e.g. 'General Physics' (J M B) or 'Properties of Matter' (C A M).

Extensions of a helical spring and *Hooke's Law*: provided the elastic limit has not been exceeded, the extension of the spring is proportional to the applied force.

Moment of a force = force × perpendicular distance between force and the fulcrum or balancing point.

The law of moments: for equilibrium, clockwise moments are equal to anticlockwise moments.

Couples: two equal and opposite forces not in the same straight line.

Centre of gravity (mass) and **stability.**

Multiple Choice Questions

Question 1 (L O N)

A metre rule whose centre of mass is at the 50 cm mark can be balanced when it is supported at the 40 cm mark provided that a downward force of 0·5 N is applied at the 20 cm mark. The weight of the metre rule is

A   0·2 N
B   0·25 N
C   0·33 N
D   0·5 N
E   1·0 N

Answer: E
A diagram will *always* help in *moments* questions. The first part of the question tells you to put the force W (weight of the ruler) at 50 cm mark. By *law of moments*:
$$0.5(N) \times 20(cm) = W(N) \times 10(cm)$$
$$W = 1.0 \text{ N}$$

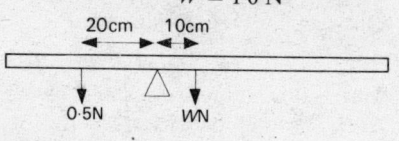

Question 2 (A E B multiple completion)
A solid right circular cone (a common cone) illustrates
1 neutral equilibrium when standing on its base
2 stable equilibrium when lying on its side
3 unstable equilibrium when balanced on its point

Answer: 3 only
1 and **2** are back to front. Visualizing the cone should suggest that it is stable when on its base.

Question 3 (L O N multiple completion)
A vertical spring was loaded with an increasing load and then unloaded again. The length of the spring varied as follows:

Load/N	Length of spring/mm Loading	Unloading
0	400	400
1	420	420
2	440	440
3	460	460
4	480	480
5	500	500

From these observations it may be deduced that

1 *Hookes Law is obeyed up to loads of 5 N*
2 *the elastic limit has not been exceeded with an extension of 100 mm*
3 *the extension for a load of 6 N would be 120 mm*

Answer: 1 and **2** only
The spring stretches 20 mm for each 1 N added, and, since the readings are unaltered on unloading, the elastic limit has not yet been reached. But we cannot predict what will happen next, as the elastic limit for this spring might be between 5 N and 6 N; so no deductions about the extension for a load of 6 N may be made.

Longer Questions

Question 1 (L O N part question)

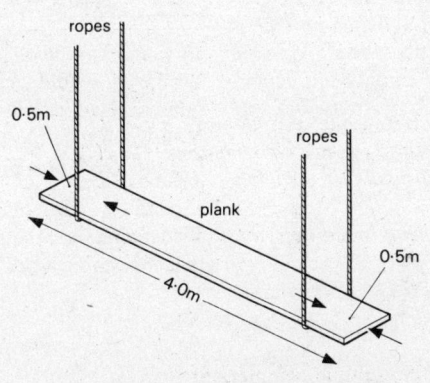

A painter stands on a uniform plank 4·0 m long and of mass 30 kg. The plank is suspended horizontally from vertical ropes attached 0·5 m from each end as shown in the diagram. The mass of the painter is 80 kg. Calculate the tensions in the ropes when the painter is 1·0 m from the centre of the platform.
(8 marks)

State briefly (no calculation required) how you would expect the tensions in the ropes to vary as the painter moves along the plank (take g = 10 N/kg).
(2 marks)

Answer

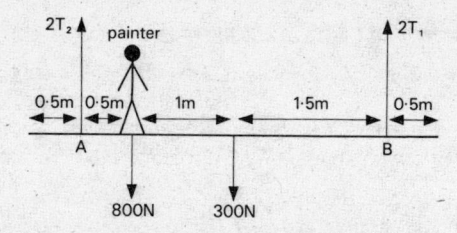

[Diagram: plank with pivot A on left and point B on right. Painter stands 0.5 m to right of A. Distances along plank: 0.5 m (left of A to end), 0.5 m (A to painter), 1 m (painter to centre), 1.5 m (centre to B), 0.5 m (B to right end). Upward forces $2T_2$ at left end and $2T_1$ at right end. Downward forces: 800 N at painter, 300 N at centre.]

The weight of the plank acts at its centre since it is uniform.
Weight of plank
   $= 30 \text{ (kg)} \times 10 \text{ (N/kg)}$
   $= 300 \text{ N}$
Weight of painter
   $= 80 \text{ (kg)} \times 10 \text{ (N/kg)}$
   $= 800 \text{ N}$
There are two ropes at each end of the plank. Let the tension in each rope at B be T_1 and at A be T_2.
Taking moments about A: since the plank is in equilibrium, clockwise moments = anticlockwise moments.
   $(800 \text{ (N)} \times 0.5 \text{ (m)}) + (300 \text{ (N)}$
         $\times 1.5 \text{ (m)})$
         $= 2T_1 \text{ (N)} \times 3 \text{ (m)}$
   $400 + 450 = 6T_1$
         $850 = 6T_1$
         $T_1 = 141\tfrac{2}{3} \text{ N}$
Since the plank is in equilibrium, upward forces = downward forces.
$2 \times 141\tfrac{2}{3} \text{ (N)} + 2T_2 \text{ (N)}$
         $= 800 \text{ (N)} + 300 \text{ (N)}$
   $283\tfrac{1}{3} + 2T_2 = 1100$
         $T_2 = 408\tfrac{1}{3} \text{ N}$
∴ the tensions in the strings are $141\tfrac{2}{3}$ N and $408\tfrac{1}{3}$ N.
As the painter moves towards B, T_1 will increase and T_2 will decrease. If he moves to A, T_1 will increase and T_2 will decrease; but $2T_1 + 2T_2 = 1100$ is always true.

Comment

Simplify the diagram.
Now explain where the numbers and distances come from.

Be careful to decide which way the moments would act if the plank were pivoted at A.
You could take moments about B, but this method is probably easier.

If you picture the painter walking on the plank, this should seem obvious.

Question 2 (AEB)

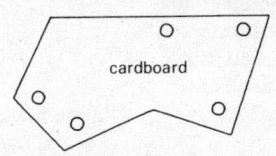

The diagram shows an irregularly shaped piece of cardboard. There are several holes in the cardboard. You are provided with a lead weight, string, suitable support stands and clamps, a needle and a rule. Describe with the aid of suitable diagrams how you would find the centre of gravity of the piece of cardboard.

Answer

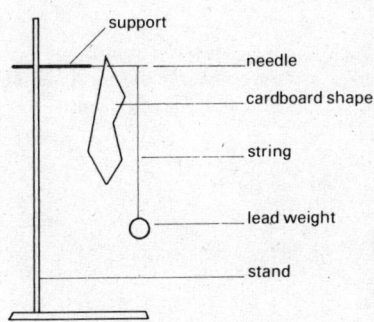

The lead weight is hung on the end of the string to act as a plumb-line and to show the vertical line. The apparatus is then set up as shown in the diagram above, with the cardboard suspended by the needle placed through one of the holes with the plumb-line in front. Having checked that the shape can hang freely, the position of the plumb-line is marked on the shape (usually with two points, which are then joined by the rule when the shape is removed from the needle). This is repeated with the shape hung from each hole in turn. The

Comment

This question comes from AEB Paper 2, which is designed to 'test familiarity with laboratory work'.

You will probably have done this experiment before, or one very similar, so think back to that.

Remember: in this paper they want lots of experimental detail, and notice the use of the plural 'diagrams' in the question.

Check that your apparatus set-up uses all the apparatus given to you.

The sort of experimental detail they want.

final result should look like the diagram below, with all the lines crossing at one point. This is the **centre of gravity** of the cardboard.

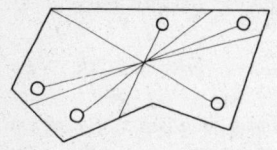

Diagrams are usually of:
(1) apparatus set up,
(2) results expected.

Remember: each line goes to a hole. Try to guess where the *centre of gravity* will be and make lines cross there.

Question 3 (LON part question)
(a) Describe how you would obtain as accurately as possible a series of readings for the load and corresponding extension of a spiral spring.
(6 marks)

(b) A student obtained the following readings:

Load/N	0	1	2	3	4	5	6
Length of spring/cm	10·0	11·5	13·0	14·5	16·0	18·5	24·0

Using these results, plot a graph of load against extension and estimate the load beyond which Hooke's law is no longer obeyed. *(7 marks)*

(c) The spring is at rest with a mass of 0·2 kg on its lower end. It is then further extended by a finger exerting a vertical force of 0·5 N. Draw a diagram showing the forces acting on the mass in this position, giving the values of the forces (take $g = 10$ m/s^2). *(3 marks)*

Answer
(a)

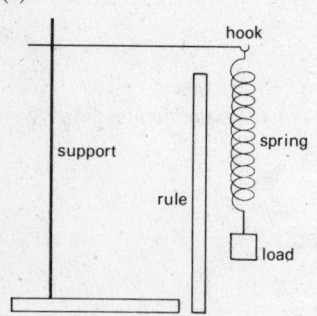

Comment

Remember: 'Describe' should at once suggest a diagram of the apparatus.

Mechanics and Properties of Matter

The apparatus is set up as shown. The length of the unloaded spring is taken, and then for each load added the corresponding length is noted. Each time the load is then removed and a reading is taken to check the spring has not been permanently stretched. The readings can also be checked when adding loads and when removing them, since more than one reading improves accuracy. For each reading the corresponding extension is worked out by subtracting the original length of the spring.

Notice that the question stresses an accurate estimate.

N.B. the question asks for the *extension* not the *length* of the spring.

(b)

Load/N	0	1	2	3	4	5	6
Length of spring/cm	10·0	11·5	13·0	14·5	16·0	18·5	24·0
Extension/cm	0	1·5	3·0	4·5	6·0	8·5	14·0

Graph of load v. extension for spring

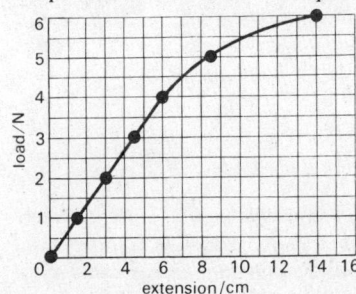

Remember to give the graph a title and labelled axes.

From the way the question is set you can expect it to be a straight line to begin with, curving as the spring is stretched.

Hooke's law is no longer obeyed beyond the 4 N load.

Don't miss this last point.

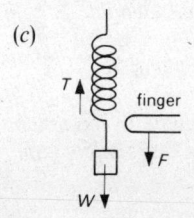

(c)

52   Passnotes: **Physics**

$F = 0.5$ N (given)
$W = 2$ N (0.2×10)
$T = 2.5$ N

Since the spring is at rest, by Newton's first law the forces on it must be balanced, i.e.

$T = W + F$

Remember: weight is the *force* not the *mass*, and weight is given by $W = mg$

Do give values for each force and explain how you find T.

Work, Energy and Power

Work = force × distance moved in the direction of the force.
(Unit: newton metre or **joule**.)
Work as transfer of **energy**.
Forms of energy and **conservation of energy** (energy cannot be created or destroyed, only changed into another form of energy).
Kinetic energy $= \frac{1}{2}mv^2$ (unit: joule).
Potential energy $= mgh$ (unit: joule).
Power is rate of working, i.e. $\dfrac{\text{work (energy) (J)}}{\text{time (s)}}$
(Unit of power: J/s or **watt**.)

Efficiency $= \dfrac{\text{useful energy obtained}}{\text{energy supplied}}$.

Multiple Choice Questions

Question 1 (A E B)
A sphere falls freely from rest at point **A** *to ground level at point* **E**. *Points* **A**, **B**, **C**, **D** *and* **E** *are equally spaced vertically. Assuming zero potential energy at* **E**, *at which point are the sphere's potential energy and kinetic energy equal?*

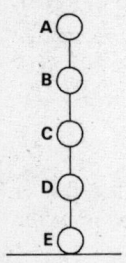

Answer: C
At **A**, all energy is *potential*.

At **E**, all energy is *kinetic*.

So **C** seems likeliest by common sense, even if you don't know your physics properly.

Mechanics and Properties of Matter 53

Question 2 (A E B)
A weight of 5 N is raised 3 m vertically whilst being moved 4 m horizontally. The work done in J is

A 15
B 20
C 25
D 35
E 60

Answer: A
The only force mentioned is *weight*, which acts vertically downward.
Work = *force × distance moved in direction of force*
  = 5 (N) × 3 (m)
  = 15 J
[Horizontal distance is included to put you off!]

Question 3 (O X F)
A boy testing his strength lifts a load of weight 30 N. The load is lifted 0·6 m 50 times in 35 seconds. Which of the following gives his power output?

A $\dfrac{50 \times 0{\cdot}6 \times 30}{35}$ W

B $\dfrac{0{\cdot}6 \times 30}{35 \times 50}$ W

C $\dfrac{30 \times 50}{0{\cdot}6 \times 35}$ W

D $\dfrac{30}{0{\cdot}6 \times 35 \times 50}$ W

E $50 \times 0{\cdot}6 \times 30 \times 35$ W

Answer: A

Power = $\dfrac{\text{work}}{\text{time}}$

Work = force × distance moved in direction of force
  = 30 × 0·6 × 50 J

power = $\dfrac{30 \times 0{\cdot}6 \times 50}{35}$ W

Question 4 (L O N)
A man is travelling across a lake in a motor boat which starts to leak. If the power of the motor remains constant, which of the alternatives listed below best describe the changes in the mass and speed of the motor boat? (Ignore the change in mass which results from the consumption of fuel by the motor.)

	Mass	Speed
A	Increases	Increases
B	Increases	Decreases
C	Decreases	Increases

Answer: B
It seems obvious to me that a leaking boat's mass increases as the water comes in!

| D | Decreases | Decreases |
| E | Increases | Unchanged |

$Power = \dfrac{work\ (energy)}{time}$, so energy ($=\frac{1}{2}mv^2$) remains constant.
If m increases, v must decrease.

Longer Questions

Question 1 (AEB part question)

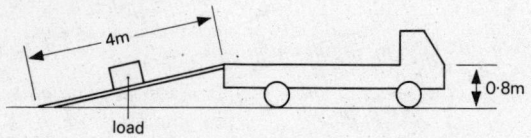

The diagram shows a loading-ramp being used to raise a load of weight 2000 N onto a lorry.
(i) How much work is done against gravity in raising the load?
(ii) Explain why the force required to move the load up the ramp is less than 2000 N.
(iii) Explain why the work done in moving the load up the ramp is greater than the work done against gravity. *(4 marks)*

Answer

(i) Work done
= force × distance moved in the direction of the force
= 2000 (N) × 0·8 (m)
= 1600 J

(ii) The force needed to pull the load up the ramp acts parallel to the ramp.
Work done by pulling force F
= F (N) × 4 (m)
2000 (N) × 0·8 (m) = F (N) × 4 (m)
∴ F < 2000 N

(iii) The work done in moving the load up the ramp (F(N) × 4(m)) will in fact be more than the work done against gravity, since there will be frictional force opposing the movement of the load up the ramp and work must be done to overcome this.

Comment

Note the last part of the definition. Weight acts vertically downwards, so the distance needed is the *vertical* distance moved.

The pulling-force acts not vertically but parallel to the ramp.

Giving the equation is probably easier than trying to explain in words.

Probably not many marks for this section, so be sure to mention friction.

Question 2 (AEB)

(a) A catapult is used to fire a stone of mass 50 g vertically to a height of 4·05 m. Calculate:
  (i) the potential energy gained by the stone,
  (ii) the speed of the stone as it leaves the catapult. *(6 marks)*

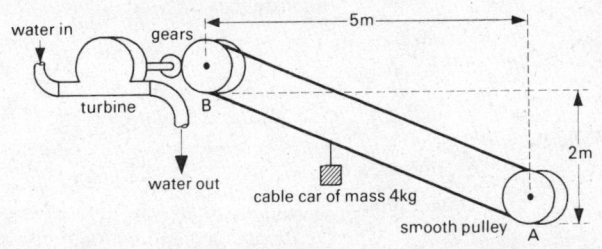

(b) The diagram shows a driving mechanism consisting of a water turbine and a set of gears. It is being used to lift a model cable car from A to B in 20 s.

Calculate:
  (i) the potential energy gained by the cable car in going from A to B,
  (ii) the output *power of the driving mechanism,*
  (iii) the input *power to the turbine, if the driving mechanism is 80% efficient. (Take* g = 10 m/s^2.) *(7 marks)*

Answer

(a) (i) Potential energy = mgh
= 0·05 (kg) × 10 (m/s^2) × 4·05 (m)
= 2·025 J

(ii) As it leaves the catapult the stone has kinetic energy, all of which is converted to potential energy;

kinetic energy = 2·025 J
= $\tfrac{1}{2}mv^2$

$\tfrac{1}{2}$ × 0·05 (kg) × v^2 (m/s)^2 = 2·025 (J)

$$v = \sqrt{\frac{2 \times 2 \cdot 025}{0 \cdot 05}}$$
= 9 m/s

Comment

Remember to use SI units.

Remember the *conservation of energy.*

(b) (i) Potential energy = mgh
   = 4 (kg) × 10 (m/s²) × 2 (m)
   = 80 J

(ii) Output power = $\dfrac{\text{energy}}{\text{time}}$

   = $\dfrac{80 \text{ (J)}}{20 \text{ (s)}}$

   = 4 W

(iii) Efficiency = $\dfrac{\text{useful power out}}{\text{power input}}$

   $0.80 = \dfrac{4}{\text{power input}}$

   power input = 5 W

Do not be put off by the complicated look of the diagram. All the turbine and gears are offputting, and are not needed for calculations. For P.E., remember it is vertical distance you need.

Remember that, though efficiency is often given as a percentage, in problems it should be converted to a decimal.

Machines

Mechanical advantage = $\dfrac{\text{load}}{\text{effort}}$

Velocity ratio = $\dfrac{\text{distance moved by effort}}{\text{distance moved by load}}$

Efficiency = $\dfrac{\text{useful work (power) out}}{\text{work (power) put in}} = \dfrac{\text{M.A.}}{\text{V.R.}}$

Effects of **friction** and methods of reducing friction.

Each board suggests specific machines to be studied, but most questions can be done from first principles. Machines include: pulley-systems, gears, levers, hydraulic press, car braking systems, screws, inclined planes. You should look at your own syllabus to see which ones you need to study particularly.

Mechanics and Properties of Matter

Multiple Choice Questions

Question 1 (AEB)
What is the velocity ratio of the machine shown?

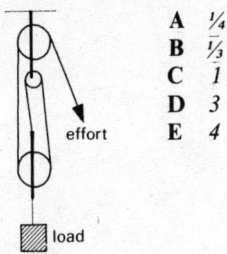

A ¼
B ⅓
C 1
D 3
E 4

Answer: D

$$\text{Velocity ratio} = \frac{\text{distance moved by effort}}{\text{distance moved by load}}$$

When load is lifted 1 cm the three strings are all shortened by 1 cm, so the effort will have to move 3 cm to take up the slack.

Question 2 (OXF)
An effort of 40 N is needed to raise a load of 120 N using a pulley-system that has a velocity ratio of 4. The efficiency of the pulley system is

A 20%
B 30%
C 40%
D 75%
E 80%

Answer D

$$\text{Mechanical advantage} = \frac{\text{load}}{\text{effort}}$$

$$\text{M.A.} = \frac{120 \text{ (N)}}{40 \text{ (N)}} = 3$$

$$\text{V.R.} = 4$$

$$\text{Efficiency} = \frac{\text{M.A.}}{\text{V.R.}} = \frac{3}{4} = 0.75$$

$$= 75\%$$

Question 3 (AEB)
In the gear train illustrated, X has 20 teeth, Y has 10 teeth and Z has 60 teeth. If X is regarded as the driving wheel, the velocity ratio of the gear train is

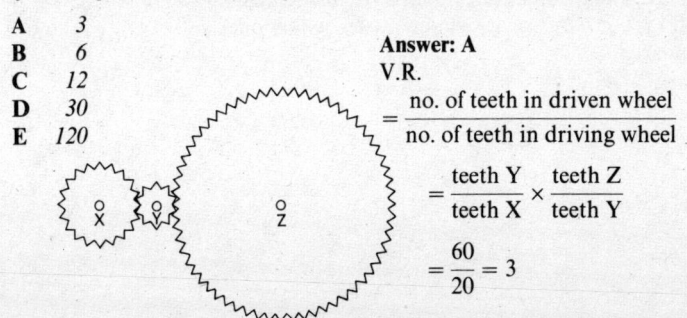

A 3
B 6
C 12
D 30
E 120

Answer: A
V.R.

$$= \frac{\text{no. of teeth in driven wheel}}{\text{no. of teeth in driving wheel}}$$

$$= \frac{\text{teeth Y}}{\text{teeth X}} \times \frac{\text{teeth Z}}{\text{teeth Y}}$$

$$= \frac{60}{20} = 3$$

Longer Questions
Question 1

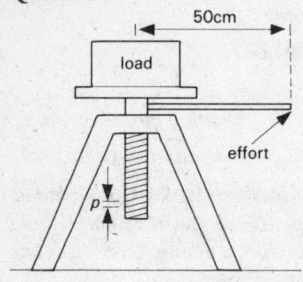

The pitch p of the screw-jack shown in the diagram is 2·0 mm. If it has a mechanical efficiency of 0·25 (25%), what is its velocity ratio? What is its mechanical advantage?

Answer

Velocity ratio = $\dfrac{\text{distance moved by effort}}{\text{distance moved by load}}$

In one revolution of the lever the load moves up through the pitch of the thread.

$$\text{V.R.} = \dfrac{2\pi \times 50 \text{ (cm)}}{0\cdot 2 \text{ (cm)}}$$

$$= 1571$$

$$\text{Efficiency} = \dfrac{\text{M.A.}}{\text{V.R.}}$$

$$0\cdot 25 = \dfrac{\text{M.A.}}{1571}$$

$$\text{M.A.} = 0\cdot 25 \times 1571$$

$$= 393$$

Comment

Pitch should be the clue here. Don't forget that the effort moves in a circle (think of doing it!)

Remember, V.R. and M.A. are *ratios*, so they have no units.

Do not give too many significant figures in your answer.

Question 2 (AEB)

(a)

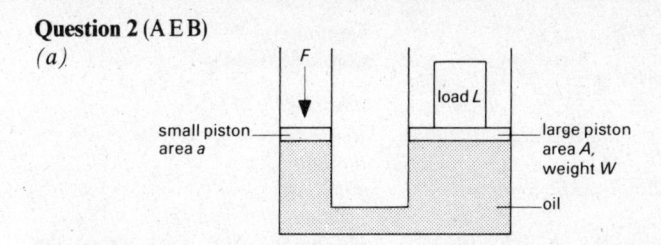

The diagram illustrates a simplified form of hydraulic press. A force F is applied to the small piston of area a and of negligible weight. Write expressions for:
  (i) the pressure exerted on the liquid by the small piston,
  (ii) the pressure exerted on the large piston,
  (iii) the force exerted by the large piston on the load L.
Indicate what becomes of the energy used in pressing down the small piston. *(7 marks)*

(b) The diagrams below illustrate a winch. An effort P is applied to the handle as shown and, as the handle turns, a rope is wound round the drum, so raising the mass M.

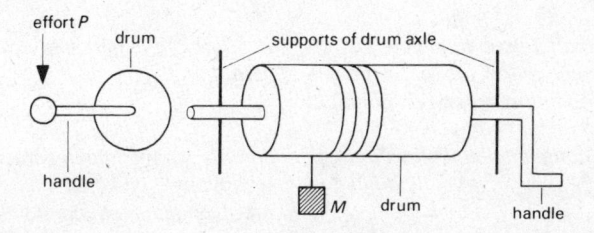

Given that the circumference of the circle in which the effort moves is 1·5 m, and that the length of the handle is three times the radius of the drum, calculate how far the mass M rises when the effort moves through one revolution.

An effort of 10 N, applied to the handle, raises a mass of 2·2 kg. Calculate:
  (i) the energy gained by the mass when the drum turns through one revolution,
  (ii) the work done by the effort during this revolution. *(7 marks)*
Suggest reasons why these two quantities are not equal. *(3 marks)*
(Take the weight of 1 kg as 10 N.)

Answer

(a) Pressure = $\dfrac{\text{force}}{\text{area}}$

(i) For small piston, pressure exerted on liquid $P_1 = \dfrac{F}{a}$

(ii) Pressure is transmitted through the liquid.
Force = pressure × area
∴ force on large piston = $P_1 \times A$

$$= \dfrac{FA}{a}$$

(iii) This force supports both the load and the weight of the piston.

$$\therefore \dfrac{FA}{a} = W + \text{force on load}$$

$$\text{force on load} = \dfrac{FA}{a} - W$$

The energy used in pressing down the small piston is used in raising the load (i.e. increasing its potential energy).

(b) Circumference of effort's circle
= 1·5 m

radius of effort's circle = $\dfrac{1\cdot 5}{2\pi}$ m

(circumference = $2\pi r$)

∴ radius of drum = $\dfrac{1\cdot 5}{6\pi}$ m

In one turn of the handle the drum moves through one circumference

∴ the mass rises $\dfrac{2\pi \times 1\cdot 5}{6\pi}$

= 0·5 m

Comment

Quote formula

This is the vital point about the hydraulic press.

Consider equilibrium of forces.

Probably few marks given, so be brief.

As with all machine problems, try to picture yourself using the machine and you should then be able to work out what is happening.

(i) Energy gained = mgh
   = 2·2 (kg) × 10 (m/s^2) × 0·5 (m)
   = 11·0 J

(ii) Work done by effort = force × distance moved in direction of force
   work = 10 (N) × 1.5 (m)
       = 15 J

These are not equal because the effort has to do work to overcome the friction of the machine, as well as to raise the load.

Use above result.

This last part is always coming up. Remember, machines are never practically 100% efficient because of friction.

Pressure

Pressure = $\dfrac{\text{Force}}{\text{Area}}$ (several possible units, e.g. N/m^2, Pascal, atmospheres, cm of mercury).

Pressure in a liquid ($p = h\rho g$ plus external pressure on the surface of the liquid).
The manometer, simple mercury barometer, aneroid barometer, piston-type air pump.
Pressure difference in a fluid as a determinant of fluid flow.

(Boyle's law and the interpretation of pressure in terms of the bombardment of molecules are dealt with under 'Heat as a form of energy. The kinetic theory', pp. 77–80).

Multiple Choice Questions

Question 1 (LON)

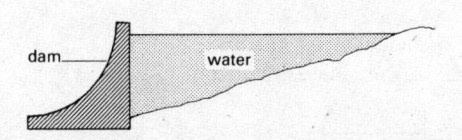

The hydrostatic pressure on the dam wall at the bottom of a deep reservoir depends on the

A depth of water
B surface area of the water
C length of the reservoir
D thickness of the dam wall
E density of the material of the dam wall

Answer: A
You know that pressure in liquids = $h\rho g$; only **A** appears in this formula.

Question 2 (AEB multiple completion)
A ballroom floor can withstand a pressure of 3000 kPa (kN/m^2) without damage. Which of the following would damage it?

1 A woman weighing 0·7 kN standing on the heel of one shoe of area 0·0001 m^2
2 An elephant weighing 200 kN standing on one foot of area 0·1 m^2
3 A 1000 kN load standing on an area of 50 m^2

Answer: 1 only

$$\text{Pressure} = \frac{\text{force}}{\text{area}}$$

1 $p = \dfrac{0.7 \text{ kN}}{0.0001 \text{ m}^2} = 7000 \text{ kPa}$

2 $p = \dfrac{200 \text{ kN}}{0.1 \text{ m}^2} = 2000 \text{ kPa}$

3 $p = \dfrac{1000 \text{ kN}}{50 \text{ m}^2} = 20 \text{ kPa}$

Now you see why stiletto heels were unpopular!

Question 3 (OXF)
The figure (not drawn to scale) represents a U-tube containing water and methylated spirit separated by mercury. The levels of the mercury in the

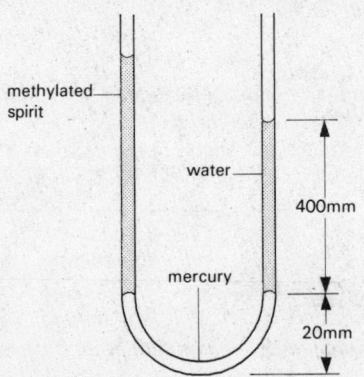

Mechanics and Properties of Matter 63

two sides are the same, 20 mm above the bottom of the U-tube. (Take the relative density of mercury to be 13·6 and that of methylated spirit to be 0·8.) If the height of the column of water above the mercury is 400 mm as shown, what is the height of the column of methylated spirit above the mercury?

A   *420 mm*
B   *500 mm*
C   *525 mm*
D   *592 mm*
E   *670 mm*

Answer B
Pressure is the same at the same level.
Pressure in a liquid = $h\rho g$
$\therefore 400 \times 1 \times g = X \times 0.8 \times g$

$$X = \frac{400}{0.8} = 500 \text{ mm}$$

A lot of distracting numbers given in this question!

Longer Questions

A vehicle designed for carrying heavy loads across mud has four wide low-pressure tyres, each of which is 120 cm wide. When the vehicle and its load have a combined mass of 12000 kg, each tyre flattens so that 50 cm of tyre is in contact with the mud as shown below.

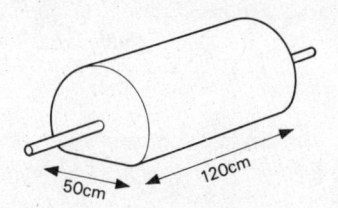

(a) Calculate
  (i) the total area of contact of the vehicle tyres with the mud,
  (ii) the pressure exerted on the mud.
(b) A car of mass 1000 kg is unable to travel across the mud although it is much lighter than the load-carrying vehicle. Why is this? (Take g = *10 N/kg.)*
(6 marks)

Answer
(a) (i) Area in contact for each tyre
  = 50 (cm) × 120 (cm)
  = 0·5 (m) × 1·2 (m)
  = 0·6 m²

Comment
Looking at the diagram should help here.

∴ total area in contact
  = 4 × 0·6 m²
  = 2·4 m²

(ii) Pressure = $\dfrac{\text{force}}{\text{area}}$

Force = weight of vehicle + load
  = 12 000 (kg) × 10 (N/kg)
  = 120 000 N

∴ pressure = $\dfrac{120\,000\ (\text{N})}{2\cdot 4\ (\text{m}^2)}$
  = 50 000 N/m²

(b) The car has tyres with a much higher air pressure in them, so the area of tyre in contact with the mud is much smaller. Even if the car is lighter than the load-carrying vehicle, therefore, it will exert a greater pressure on the mud and be unable to drive across it.

Don't forget there are *four* tyres.

N.B. force = weight here and the question only gives you mass, so do remember to convert it using the formula weight = mass × *g*.

Think about a car and you should realize that the tyres don't look like the diagram above, so it is likely that this section is about reduced area of contact and therefore increased pressure.

Question 2 (AEB part question)

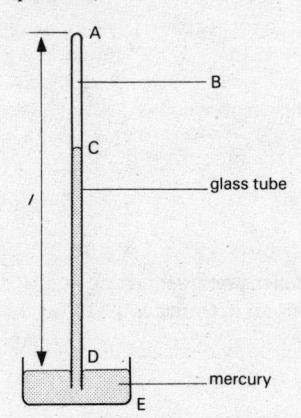

The diagram shows an instrument which is used to measure the pressure of the atmosphere.
(i) Name the instrument.
(ii) State a reasonable value for l, in m.

Mechanics and Properties of Matter 65

(iii) What would you expect to find in the space B?
(iv) What measurement would you take in order to calculate the pressure of the atmosphere?
(v) Show how you would use this measurement to calculate the pressure of the atmosphere, in Pa, explaining any symbols used.

Answer	**Comment**
(i) The mercury barometer.	'Name', so don't go into details.
(ii) *l* should be about 1·20 m.	If you look at the diagram you can see the mercury level is about two-thirds of the way up the tube. As you expect this height to be about 76 cm, the height of the tube must be about 120 cm. N.B. the question asks for the answer in metres.
(iii) A vacuum.	
(iv) The height CD.	You should remember having seen this demonstrated.
(v) The pressure of the atmosphere supports the column of mercury.	
∴ atmospheric pressure $= h\rho g$ where	
$h =$ CD (m)	
$\rho =$ density of mercury (kg/m^3)	
$g =$ acceleration due to gravity (m/s^2)	Be careful to say what the units should be.
If the units are as shown above, the pressure will be in Pa.	

Flotation

Archimedes' Principle: when a body is totally or partially immersed in a fluid it experiences an upthrust equal to the weight of fluid displaced.

Flotation: a floating body displaces an amount of fluid whose weight is equal to the weight of the body.

Bulb and stem hydrometer.

Multiple Choice Questions

Question 1 (AEB)

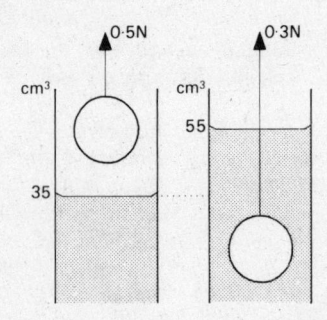

A glass sphere weighs 0·5 N in air and 0·3 N when totally immersed in water. If the density of water is 1·0 g/cm³ and the acceleration of free fall is 10 m/s², the density of glass in g/cm³ is

A   0·40
B   0·60
C   1·50
D   1·67
E   2·50

Answer: E

(g – acceleration due to gravity)

weight in water = weight in air − upthrust

upthrust = 0·5 N − 0·3 N = 0·2 N

By *Archimedes' principle*, upthrust = wt of liquid displaced

Wt of liquid displaced = vol. of sphere × density of water × g

$$0.2 \text{ N} = v \times 1.0 \text{ (g/cm}^3) \times g$$

Wt in air = vol. of sphere × density of glass × g

$$0.5 \text{ N} = v \times d \text{ (g/cm}^3) \times g$$

$$0.5 = \frac{0.2 \times d \times g}{1.0 \times g}$$

$$d = \frac{0.5}{0.2} = 2.50 \text{ g/cm}^3$$

Question 2 (AEB)

A hollow glass sphere of mass 60 g floats in water so that two thirds of its external volume is under water of density 1 g/cm³. The volume in cm³ of the sphere is

A 16
B 24
C 40
D 66
E 90

Answer: E

By *Archimedes' Principle*, upthrust = wt of water displaced

By *law of flotation*, upthrust = wt of sphere

$60 \times g$ = wt of liquid displaced

Wt of liquid displaced = mass of liquid $\times g$
= vol. of liquid × density of liquid $\times g$
= vol. of sphere in liquid × density of liquid $\times g$

(Since objects displace their own volume – think of yourself getting into a bath!)

$60 \times g = \tfrac{2}{3}v \times 1 \times g$

$\therefore v = 90 \text{ cm}^3$

Question 3 (LON multiple completion)
A hydrometer sinks to a greater depth in water than in a certain liquid L. From this it can be concluded that:

1 *the density of L is greater than that of water.*
2 *the expansivity of L is smaller than that of water*
3 *the hydrometer displaces a greater mass of water than of L*

Answer: 1 only
This is the principle of the hydrometer.
2 is obviously just a distractor.
3 cannot be true since the hydrometer is floating in both cases, and so, by the *law of flotation*, must displace the same weight (or mass) of liquid each time.

Longer Questions

Question 1 (AEB)
A cube of wood of volume 0.2 m^3 and density 600 kg/m^3 is placed in a liquid of density 800 kg/m^3.
   (i) What fraction of the volume of the wood would be immersed in the liquid?

(ii) What force must be applied to the cube so that the top surface of the cube is on the same level as the liquid surface?
(Take $g = 10$ m/s^2.)

Answer
(i) Let a volume V^1 of the cube be immersed in the liquid.

Weight of liquid displaced =
$$V^1 \text{ (m}^3\text{)} \times 800 \text{ (kg/m}^3\text{)} \times g \text{ (m/s}^2\text{)}$$

By **law of flotation**:

wt of liquid displaced = wt of cube
$$V^1 \times 800 \times g = 0.2 \times 600 \times g$$

$$V^1 = \frac{120 \text{ m}^3}{800} = 0.15 \text{ m}^3$$

∴ fraction immersed $= \dfrac{V^1}{V} = \dfrac{0.15}{0.2}$

$$= 0.75$$

(ii) In order that all the cube is immersed,

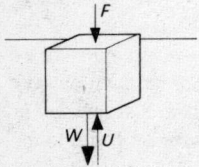

Comment
Since only a fraction of the wood is immersed, it must be floating; so think of *law of flotation.*

A quick diagram will help you to think what is actually happening.

Force pushing down = upthrust
  − weight

F = wt of liquid displaced
  − weight of cube
 $= 0.2 \times 800 \times g - 0.2 \times 600 \times g$
 $= 0.2 \times 200 \times g$
 $= 400$ N

Mechanics and Properties of Matter 69

Question 2 (LON)

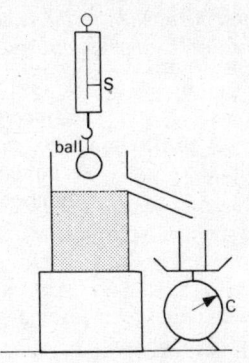

A solid metal ball is suspended from the spring balance S as shown so that it is just above the surface of the water in the displacement can. The spout of the can is just above an empty beaker, which rests on a compression balance C.
Describe how the readings of both balances will alter as
(a) the ball is lowered slowly until it is just below the surface of the water, and
(b) the ball is now lowered slowly until it rests on the bottom of the displacement can. (6 marks)
Draw a diagram of the ball showing the forces acting on the ball when it is at rest just below the surface of the water. What is the relationship between these forces? (5 marks)
State and explain how (if at all) the readings of S and C would vary, if the displacement can contained a liquid whose density was less than that of water. (3 marks)
If the reading of the spring balance is 7·0 N when the ball is suspended in air and 6·2 N when it is fully submerged in water, calculate the relative density of the material of the ball. (6 marks)

Answer
(a) As the ball is submerged in the water, water is displaced into the beaker, so the reading on C increases as the ball is lowered below the surface. *Archimedes' Principle* states that if a body is totally or partially immersed in a fluid, it experiences an upthrust equal to the weight of fluid displaced. The

Comment
Think practically what happens, i.e. water pours out of the spout, so C must go up.

It's worth quoting Archimedes' Principle here, as you are going to use it a great deal in this question.

upthrust therefore gradually increases as more and more of the ball is submerged, so the value of S gradually decreases. We expect the final amount by which S has decreased to be equal to the amount by which C has increased.
(b) As the ball is lowered in the liquid no more water is displaced, since it is already completely submerged. The readings on C and S will therefore stay steady until the ball rests on the bottom of the can, when S will read 0.

The last part shows that you understand Archimedes' Principle.

When the ball is on the bottom it is totally supported, so S must go back to zero. You can picture yourself doing this: it will then seem obvious.

W – weight of ball
T gives reading on S
U – upthrust

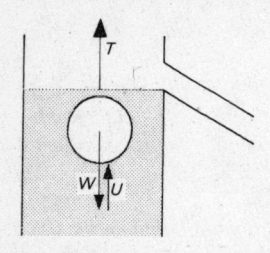

$T + U = W$, since the ball is in equilibrium.
If the liquid in the can was of a density less than water, the volume of liquid displaced would be the same but its mass and weight would be less; the final reading on C would therefore be less, and S would reduce by a correspondingly smaller amount.

The ball is stationary and all forces are vertical, so they must balance.
Mass = density × volume, so if volume is the same and density less, mass would be less.
Mass ∝ weight.

$$\text{Weight in air} = 7{\cdot}0 \text{ N}$$
$$\text{Weight in water} = 6{\cdot}2 \text{ N}$$
$$\therefore \text{ upthrust} = 0{\cdot}8 \text{ N}$$
$$\text{Let volume of ball} = V \text{ m}^3$$
$$V \times \text{density ball} \times g = 7{\cdot}0 \text{ N}$$

Mechanics and Properties of Matter 71

By Archimedes' Principle:
$V \times$ density water $\times g = 0{\cdot}8$ N
Relative density of ball

$$= \frac{\text{density of ball}}{\text{density of water}}$$

$$= \frac{7{\cdot}0}{0{\cdot}8}$$

$$= 8{\cdot}75$$

Relative density is a ratio, so it has no units.

General Questions

It is easy to make up questions that test several aspects of this part of the syllabus at once, especially in longer questions, so you will often find mixed questions. Some concepts, e.g. friction, are rarely tested on their own, but do crop up in this way.

Multiple Choice Questions

J M B and London set a kind of multiple choice question called a matching pairs question, which always tests several ideas; here is an example.

Question 1 (L O N)
The following are five vector quantities:

A *acceleration*
B *displacement*
C *momentum*
D *velocity*
E *weight*
   Which of these
   (i) is measured in newtons?
   (ii) will tell you most about how difficult it will be to bring a moving body to rest?
   (iii) can be calculated from the product (average velocity) × (time) for a uniform accelerated motion in a straight line?

Answer
(i) **E**: the only force in the list.
(ii) **C**: 'how difficult' is presumably asking about the force needed, and force = change in momentum/time.
(iii) **B**: average velocity $= \dfrac{v+u}{2}$,
and $s = \frac{1}{2}(u+v)t$
or average speed $= \dfrac{\text{distance}}{\text{time}}$
∴ distance = (average speed) × (time)

72   *Passnotes:* **Physics**

Some questions are not easily categorized, as the following demonstrate.

Question 2 (AEB)
The total mass of a balloon containing hydrogen may be decreased by

1 *letting out some hydrogen*
2 *taking it up a mountain*
3 *placing it in a vacuum*

Answer: 1 only
Remember, *mass* is connected to number of molecules present, and **2** and **3** will not affect this.

Question 3 (LON)
The diagram represents a simple pendulum making small oscillations between positions P and R. At position Q the bob has maximum

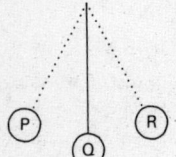

1 *potential energy*
2 *velocity*
3 *momentum*

Answer: 2 and **3** only
Potential energy depends on height, so as Q is in the lowest position this is unlikely. Since *momentum* is mass × velocity, if **2** is true **3** must be true as well.

Longer Questions

Question 1 (OXF)
A child's gun fires a cork of mass 60 g by means of a compressed spring. The spring is 100 mm long and is compressed to 60 mm when loading the gun. The stored energy in the compressed spring is 3 J.
(a) What is the greatest speed at which the cork could leave the gun?
(4 marks)
(b) The cork is fired horizontally at a height of 1 m above the ground. Neglecting air resistance, calculate the horizontal distance that the cork travels before hitting the ground. *(4 marks)*
(c) Would it make any difference to the time of flight or to the horizontal range if air resistance was not negligible? Explain. *(4 marks)*
(d) Describe an experiment that could be carried out with the spring removed from the gun to find out how the force exerted by the spring depends on its length. How does the force on the cork vary during firing?
(6, 2 marks)

Answer
(a) If all the energy of the spring were given to the cork:

energy $= \frac{1}{2}mv^2$

Comment
A lot of information is given about the spring. You have to choose what will be most useful.

$3(J) = \frac{1}{2}(60 \times 10^{-3})(kg) \times v^2 \, (m/s)^2$

$v^2 = \dfrac{6}{60 \times 10^{-3}}$

$v = 10$ m/s

For *energy* definitions see p. 52.
Be careful of units.

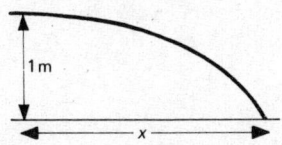

(b) The cork falls 1 m while travelling x m horizontally

Vertically: $u = 0 \quad s = 1$ m
$\qquad a = 10 \text{ m/s}^2 \quad t = ?$
$\qquad s = ut + \frac{1}{2}at^2$
$\qquad 1 = 0 + \frac{1}{2} \times 10 \times t^2$
$\qquad t = \sqrt{0.2}$ s

Motion in a straight line; see p. 32.

Horizontally there is no acceleration:
Distance = speed × time
$\quad u = 10$ m/s $\quad t = \sqrt{0.2}$ s $\quad s = x$
$\quad x = 10 \times \sqrt{0.2}$ m
$\quad\;\; = 4.47$ m

(c) If there were air resistance a force would act to oppose the motion of the cork. This would produce a backward acceleration in the direction the cork is moving (i.e. with horizontal and vertical components), so both the time of flight and the horizontal range would be affected.

By *Newton's second law*, an unbalanced force always produces an *acceleration*. Friction always acts to oppose motion, so it would affect both parts of the calculation in (b) above.

(d) For experiment, see answer to Question 3, p. 50.
The force exerted on the bullet is greatest when the spring is most compressed and lessens as the spring unwinds, since force ∝ compression.

Use the figures given in the first part for discussion of the experiment.

Think of squashing a spring and you will 'feel' how force changes as you do so.

Question 2 (LON)
(a)

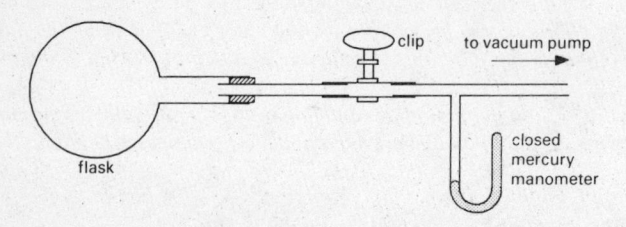

The diagram illustrates the apparatus for an experiment in which the density of air is to be determined.

   (i) Describe briefly how the volume of the flask could be measured.
(3 marks)

   (ii) List the readings which must be taken before the mass of air in the flask can be calculated. (2 marks)

   (iii) During the determination it is necessary to remove all the air from the flask. How does the experimenter know that this has been done?
(2 marks)

   (iv) It is usual to measure the atmospheric pressure and also the room temperature when determining the density of air, but not when determining the density of a solid. Why is this necessary? (1 mark)

(b) A balloon has a volume of 2·0 m³ when filled with helium. The mass of the balloon fabric is 0·24 kg. A long coiled rope of mass per unit length 0·14 kg/m rests on the ground with one end attached to the balloon; as the balloon rises the rope uncoils as shown below.

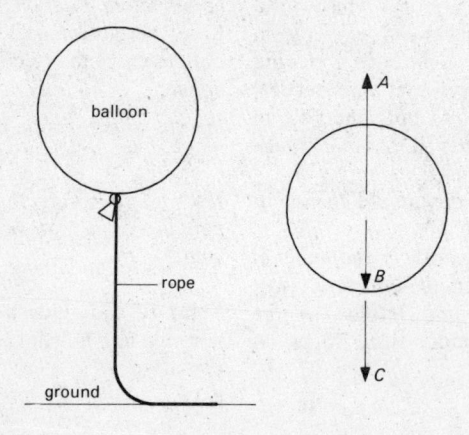

Mechanics and Properties of Matter 75

(i) The right-hand diagram shows the forces acting on the balloon when it stops rising. Name the forces **A**, **B** and **C**. *(4 marks)*

(ii) What is the relationship between these forces? *(1 mark)*

(iii) Calculate the length of rope which has uncoiled when the balloon has stopped rising. (Density of helium = 0.13 kg/m^3. Density of air = 1.30 kg/m^3.) *(4 marks)*

(iv) If the rope is now allowed to fall away from the balloon, the balloon again rises and eventually bursts. Explain why the balloon bursts.
(3 marks)

Answer

(a) (i) The volume of the flask could be measured by filling it with water; this is poured out into a measuring cylinder and the volume of water, which is the same as that of the flask, can then be found.

(ii) Mass of flask when full of air + clip + bung + tubing (so that when air is removed the new weight can be found and subtracted).

(iii) When all the air has been removed there will be a vacuum in the flask, so the level of mercury in the two arms of the manometer will be equal.

(iv) The volume of a gas depends on its pressure and temperature, while that of a solid varies much less with changes of pressure and temperature.

(b) (i) *A* – upthrust
 B – weight of balloon + helium
 C – weight of uncoiled rope

(ii) As balloon has stopped rising it is in equilibrium, ∴ $A = B + C$.

Comment

N.B. 'Briefly', so don't give lots of detail.
Choose any easy method.

Only 2 marks, so just think of doing the experiment yourself.

The manometer must be there for some purpose and it's not much help as shown in the diagram, so think how it will move as pressure is reduced in the flask.

Only 1 mark, so don't go into much detail.

B operates on the balloon from its centre, so it is probably its weight. Remember, *C* is only for rope that has uncoiled; the rest is still supported on the ground (examiners were disappointed at how few candidates mentioned *upthrust*)

(iii) By Archimedes' Principle:
upthrust = wt of fluid displaced
weight = volume × density × g
$A = 2.0 \,(m^3) \times 1.30 \,(kg/m^3) \times 10 \,(m/s^2) = 26$ N

$B = 2.0 \,(m^3) \times 0.13 \,(kg/m^3) \times 10 \,(m/s^2) = 2.6$ N

$\therefore C = 26 - 2.6 = 23.4$ N

Let length of uncoiled rope = X (m)
Weight of rope = 23.4 N =
X (m) × 0.14 (kg/m) × 10 (m/s²)
23.4 = 1.4 X
X = 16.7 m

(iv) When the rope falls away, $A > B$, so the balloon rises. The pressure lessens as the balloon rises, so the volume of helium increases $\left(\dfrac{p_1 V_1}{T_1} = \dfrac{p_2 V_2}{T_2}\right)$ and the balloon will eventually burst as the balloon fabric becomes too weak to expand further.

This question encourages you to use their forces as suggested in their diagram.

For *gas laws*, see p. 95.
There will be both pressure and temperature changes as the balloon rises, but *pressure* will be more important (examiners reported this part to be very poorly done).

Section 4: Heat

Heat as a Form of Energy. The Kinetic Theory

Heat is a measure of the internal **energy** of a system and is measured in joules. It can be converted to and from other forms of energy.

The **kinetic theory** states that the average velocity of molecules (and therefore their **kinetic energy**) is proportional to the temperature of the substance.

When a substance changes state the **potential energy** of the molecules changes.

The pressure exerted by a gas is caused by the collision of molecules against its containing walls.

Multiple Choice Questions

Question 1 (AEB)
Which of the following properties of a body is most directly related to the average kinetic energy of its molecules?

A Heat capacity
B Specific heat capacity
C Linear expansivity
D Temperature
E Thermal conductivity

Answer: D
The mention of 'kinetic energy of molecules' should make you think of the *kinetic theory* at once.

Question 2 (LON)
If a fixed mass of gas is compressed at constant temperature the molecules of the gas will

A have more kinetic energy
B have more momentum
C hit the sides of the container more often
D move faster
E move more slowly

Answer: C
N.B. 'constant temperature': you must think at once that this means *constant velocity*.
C is the only answer that does not include velocity.
(K.E. = $\frac{1}{2}mv^2$; momentum = mv)

Question 3 (LON multiple completion)
In the observation of Brownian motion the observed particles

1 *are larger than the molecules of the fluid*
2 *have an average speed which is less than that of the molecules of the fluid*
3 *appear as dark specks against a light background*

Answer: 1 and 2
Brownian motion shows large particles being bombarded by invisible molecules and so moving slowly. They are viewed under a microscope and are seen as *bright* specks.

Longer Questions

Question 1 (LON)
Explain the following on the basis of the motion of molecules.

(a) When a liquid is caused to evaporate rapidly by a current of air the remaining liquid is cooled. (4 marks)
(b) The pressure of a fixed mass of gas which is enclosed in a container of constant volume increases if its temperature is raised. (4 marks)

Answer
(*a*) The molecules of a gas have a higher average velocity than those of the liquid state of the same substance. In a liquid the molecules move with a range of velocities, some of them fast enough to be a gas, while some slower-moving molecules from the gas (vapour) above condense back into liquid. This **dynamic equilibrium** is destroyed by the current of air which removes the gas molecules. The **kinetic theory** states that the average velocity of molecules is proportional to their temperature. When the air removes the faster-moving molecules the average velocity of those left behind is slower, and this means a lower temperature.
(*b*) As the average temperature of the gas is raised the average

Comment
Answer plan
(1) Molecules of a liquid are *slower* on *average* than those of a gas.
(2) *Dynamic equilibrium* normally exists between vapour and liquid.
(3) State the kinetic theory.
(4) Discuss the effect of the current of air.

velocity of the molecules increases, according to the kinetic theory. The molecules collide with each other and with the walls of the container, rebounding and thus changing their momentum (mass × velocity).

Force = rate of change of momentum

Pressure = $\dfrac{\text{force}}{\text{area}}$

As the momentum of the molecules increases with increasing temperature *and* they collide more often with the walls of the container, the pressure of the gas will increase.

Answer plan
(1) Restate the kinetic theory.
(2) Pressure is related to molecular movement.
(3) Quote relevant formulae.
(4) Show how increased velocity increases pressure.

Question 2 (LON part question)
(a) Explain in terms of the kinetic theory:

(i) the behaviour of the molecules in a material which is changing from the solid state to the liquid state,
(ii) why a gas exerts a pressure on its containing vessel,
(iii) the cooling of a liquid when evaporation occurs. *(8 marks)*

(b) Describe what is meant by Brownian motion. *(3 marks)*
(c) If you wish to demonstrate Brownian motion:

(i) name the materials you would use,
(ii) state how they are contained,
(iii) describe how you would observe the motion,
(iv) describe what you would observe. *(5 marks)*

Answer
The kinetic theory states that the average velocity of molecules is proportional to their temperature.
(*a*) (i) When a material is changing from the solid state to the liquid state its temperature remains constant, so the kinetic energy of the molecules remains the same.

Comment
Quote kinetic theory at start of question, then use it to answer (*a*).

Change of state – you should immediately think of constant temperature. So K.E. is unchanged, but P.E. changes.

Molecules in a solid vibrate about fixed positions, whereas those in a liquid move faster and more freely because they are more widely separated; so their potential energy is increased.

(ii) and (iii): see Question 1 above.

(*b*) Brownian motion is the movement of relatively large molecules (e.g. smoke) as they are battered by fast-moving, much smaller molecules (e.g. air) which are too small to be seen.

Only 3 marks, so be clear but not too detailed.

(*c*) (i) Smoke molecules and air molecules.

(ii) In a small glass cell with microscope slide as cover.

(iii)

'Name', 'State' – do not bother to go into detail.

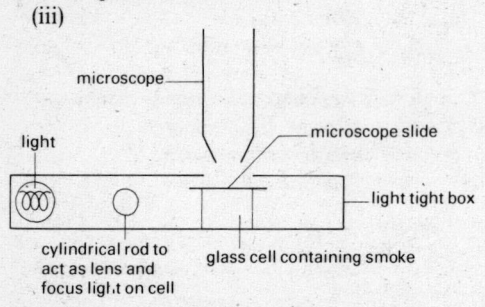

[Diagram: microscope positioned above a light tight box containing a glass cell with smoke; microscope slide as cover; light source on left with cylindrical rod to act as lens and focus light on cell.]

The cell is illuminated, and the light reflected off the smoke molecules is viewed through a microscope.

(iv) Bright specks are to be seen moving randomly in all directions.

'Describe' – a diagram will often save time and help clarify your answer.

Heat 81

Measurement of Temperature

Celsius and **Kelvin** scales. Fixed points and experiments to determine these.
Mercury thermometer and clinical thermometer.
(Constant volume gas thermometer will be considered in 'Expansion of gases and the gas laws', pp. 95–102.)
This section is mostly descriptive and easy-to-learn bookwork.

Multiple Choice Questions

Question 1 (LON)
The fact that the level of the mercury in a mercury-in-glass thermometer rises when the temperature is raised shows that

A mercury is a good radiator of heat
B glass is a poor conductor of heat
C glass does not expand when heated
D glass expands less than mercury when heated
E mercury expands uniformly with rise in temperature

Answer: D
Several of these answers contain true facts, but only **D** completes the sentence.

Question 2 (AEB)
A temperature scale X has an ice point of 40° and steam point of 240°. What is the temperature in °X when the Celsius temperature is 50°C?

A 80
B 100
C 120
D 140
E 160

Answer: D
The problem is a numerical one.
Celsius ice point = 0°C
Celsius steam point = 100°C

$$\frac{50-0}{100-0} = \frac{x-40}{240-40}$$

$$x = 140$$

Question 3 (LON multiple completion)
Which of the following is (are) characteristic of a clinical thermometer?

1 Constriction in the bore
2 Limited scale
3 Alcohol filled

Answer: 1 and 2
(Common experience should allow you to guess this answer!)

Longer Questions

Question 1 (LON)

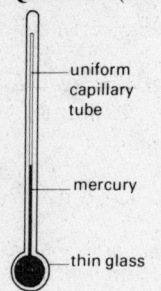

(a) You are provided with an uncalibrated thermometer as shown here. The mercury level is about one quarter of the way up the stem at room temperature. Describe how you would calibrate the instrument by marking two fixed points and then use it to determine room temperature. *(12 marks)*

Thermometer diagram labels: uniform capillary tube; mercury; thin glass.

(b) Explain why, in the above instrument,

(i) the glass surrounding the bulb is thin even though this makes it fragile, *(2 marks)*

(ii) the mercury level will not immediately rise to its final steady level when the thermometer is placed in a warm liquid. *(2 marks)*

(c) Explain why

(i) an alcohol-filled thermometer might be preferred to a mercury-filled one by an Arctic explorer, *(2 marks)*

(ii) in a clinical thermometer the bulb is not quite full of mercury at room temperature. *(2 marks)*

Answer

(a) The lower fixed point on a Celsius thermometer is the temperature of pure melting ice (0°C).

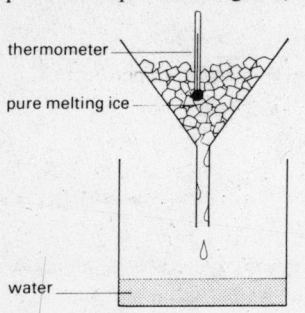

Diagram labels: thermometer; pure melting ice; water.

Comment

The allocation of marks shows that part (a) is the most important. Diagrams are essential in any experimental description.

Answer plan
(1) Explain fixed points.
(2) Ice point.
(3) Steam point.
(4) Scale.
(5) Room temperature measurement.

The mercury level must show above the ice. It is marked after it has remained steady for a time.

(Since at room temperature ($\simeq 20°$) the mercury is a quarter of the way up the stem, the level will not fall into the bulb at 0°C.)

The part in brackets is not essential to the answer, but it will show the examiner that you have read the question and have a practical knowledge of temperature.

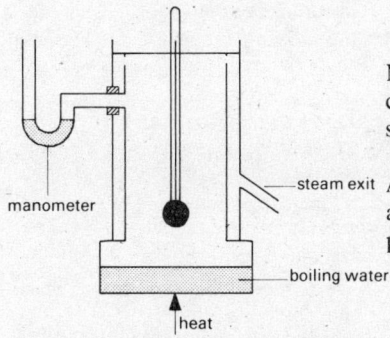

Make sure the thermometer is clearly above water level and in the steam.

As pressure is important, include a manometer to show that the pressure inside is atmospheric.

The upper fixed point is the temperature of steam from water boiling under standard atmospheric pressure (100°C). The bulb of the thermometer is kept above the boiling water to be in the steam. The manometer should show an equal level in each arm to check that pressure inside the apparatus is atmospheric. When the thermometer has been left for some time and the mercury level is steady, it is marked on the stem (it must be higher than the cork in the apparatus).

The distance between the two marks represents 100°C, so it is divided equally into 100 parts. The

N.B. (1) Steady temperature.
     (2) Mark level.

thermometer is then allowed to stand at room temperature until it is steady and the temperature is then read off.

(b) (i) Glass is a poor conductor of heat, and it must be thin to allow the heat to reach the mercury quickly, which can then respond promptly to changes in temperature.

(ii) Both the conduction of heat to the mercury and through it will take time, so the response will not be immediate.

(c) (i) Mercury freezes at $-39°C$, and temperatures in the Arctic may easily be lower than this. Alcohol freezes at $-115°C$, so it is more suitable for low-temperature regions.

(ii) The clinical thermometer has a limited range around the body's normal temperature ($37°C$). Since room temperature is $\simeq 20°C$, the mercury will have shrunk back into the bulb which will not be full of mercury.

Now check answer plan, and see that you have included everything.

Only 2 marks, so a short answer is enough.

Again, only 2 marks.

Don't worry if you can't remember exact freezing points; just remember that mercury freezes at a higher temperature than alcohol.

Two important points about clinical thermometer:
(a) constriction in bore, and
(b) limited range;
so you expect one of these to be the explanation.

Transfer of Thermal Energy

Conduction, **convection** and **radiation**. (You need to be able to describe each of these processes and to recognize which is taking place in any particular transfer of energy.)
Vacuum flask.
House insulation.

Multiple Choice Questions

Question 1 (L O N)
Which of the following processes is the best illustration of heat transfer by conduction?

A   From a boiler to a hot-water tank
B   From a hot flame to a saucepan
C   From an electric fire to a person sitting in front of it
D   From the hot surface of a metal radiator to the rest of the room
E   Through the glass of a greenhouse

Answer: B
Conduction should make you think at once of heat transfer in *solids*.

Question 2 (A E B)
In cold weather the metal blade of a knife feels cooler than the wooden handle because the

A   metal is at a lower temperature than the wood
B   metal is a better conductor of heat than wood
C   metal has a smaller specific heat capacity than wood
D   metal has a brighter surface than the wood
E   molecules in the metal are vibrating more vigorously than those in the wood

Answer: B
At same temperature, **A** and **E** *must* be wrong. Since both wood and metal are solids, *conduction* should spring to mind.

Question 3 (L O N multiple completion)
The space between the walls of a vacuum flask is evacuated to reduce heat loss by

1   conduction
2   convection
3   radiation

Answer: 1 and **2**
Radiation is the *only* form of heat transfer across a vacuum.

Question 4 (A E B)

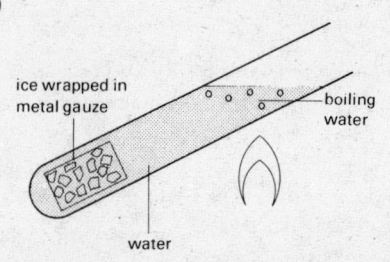

A piece of ice is wrapped in copper gauze at the bottom of a boiling-tube containing water. The water at the top can be boiled by heating as shown, while the ice remains frozen. Which of the following statements best explains this?

A   Most of the heat given to the water is lost by evaporation.
B   Convection currents are set up and the descending cold water keeps the ice cold.
C   The copper gauze conducts heat away from the ice.
D   A lot of heat is required to melt ice.
E   Water and glass are poor conductors of heat.

Answer: E
Obviously a question of heat transfer, so likely to be **B**, **C** or **E**.

D is unlikely because of the unscientific phrase 'a lot of'.

Longer Questions

Question 1 (L O N)
(a) Describe an experiment which you would carry out to show how the nature of a surface affects the heat radiated from the surface in a given time. (5 marks)
State any precautions which you would take and state your finding for two named surfaces. (3 marks)
How would you then show that the surface which was the better radiator was also the better absorber of radiation? (4 marks)
(b) As the surface of a pond freezes, it is found that each equal increase in the thickness of the ice takes longer to form even when the air above the ice remains at the same low temperature. Explain why this is so.
(4 marks)

(c) (Diagram as in Question 4 above.) In the experiment shown in the diagram the ice remains intact for several minutes as heating progresses. Explain how this can be so. *(4 marks)*

Answer
(a)

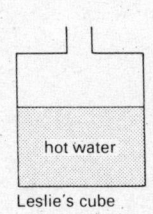

```
    ┌──┐  ┌──┐
    │  │  │  │
    ├──┴──┴──┤
    │░░░░░░░░│
    │hot water│
    │░░░░░░░░│
    └────────┘
   Leslie's cube
```

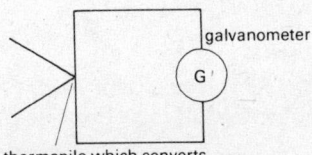

```
              galvanometer
   \          ┌─────┐
    \         │  G  │
   ──┤        └─────┘
    /
   /
```
thermopile which converts
heat energy to electrical energy

Leslie's cube is a hollow cube each side of which is a different surface (polished metal, blackened matt metal, white paint, shiny black paint). The amount of heat radiated is measured by the deflection of the galvanometer.

The temperature of the water must be kept constant and the thermopile must be put at the same distance from each side of the cube.

We expect dull black to give the highest reading and polished metal the lowest.

Four plates – with surfaces as overleaf – have a cork held on their backs by wax. They are held equidistant from a heat source and the cork slips off the dull black plate first, showing that it is the best absorber of heat.

Comment
                Answer plan
(1) Diagram (essential).
(2) Method.
(3) Precautions.
(4) Answers for two named surfaces.

(1) Be sure you are clear about *radiation* and *absorption*.

(2) It is a help to remember all four surfaces.

(3)

(4)

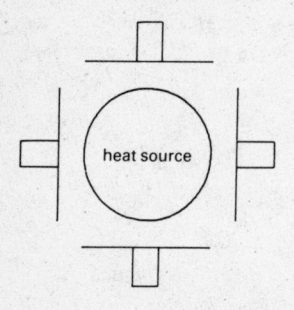

(b) Ice is a poor conductor of heat, so the thicker the ice is, the longer it takes for the temperature change to be transferred to the liquid and the ice to be formed.

The thickness of the ice is what is changing, so this should suggest *conduction* to you.

(c) Heat is transferred to the water from the flame. Both glass and water are poor conductors of heat. Any **convection** currents pass the heat upwards in the liquid. Copper is a good conductor of heat, so any heat that does reach the ice is carried away by the copper, and it takes some time for the ice to melt.

Consider how heat could reach the ice and why this should be slow.

Question 2 (LON)
A person sitting on a beach on a calm, hot summer's day is aware of a cool breeze blowing from the sea. Explain why there is a breeze.

Answer
The breeze is caused by a *convection* current set up between the sea and the land.
The specific heat capacity of sea water is much higher than the specific heat capacity of the land. Since the rate of heat energy supplied is the same for sea and land, and heat energy = S.H.C. × mass × change in temperature, the

Comment
Breeze or wind should suggest
(*a*) pressure changes or
(*b*) convection currents.
(*Convection* is the vital word and idea here.)

See 'Specific heat capacity', p. 103.

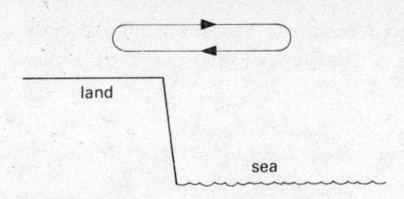

land will be quicker to warm up than the sea.
Since the land is warmer than the sea, the air above the land expands, becomes less dense and rises, while cold air from the sea comes in to take its place.

Expansion of Solids and Liquids

Experiment to find **linear expansivity** of a metal.
Formulae: $l = l_0(1 + \alpha\theta)$ and $e = l_0\alpha\theta$ (with usual symbols).
Practical examples of **expansion**.
Bimetallic strip.
Expansion of liquids and unusual expansion of water.

Multiple Choice Questions

Question 1 (AEB)
The length of a metal rod is 100 cm and the linear expansivity (coefficient of linear expansion) of the metal is 0·00002/K. By how many centimetres will it contract when cooled through 50 K?

A   1·001
B   0·150
C   0·100
D   0·050
E   0·001

Answer: C
$e = l_0\alpha\theta$
   = 100 (cm) × 0·00002/K × 50 (K)
   = 0·1 cm

Question 2 (AEB multiple completion)
During an experiment to measure the expansivity of a rod or tube which of the following measurements are necessary?

1 *The length before heating*
2 *The change in length during heating*
3 *The change in temperature*

Answer: 1, 2 and 3
Since $l = l_0(1 + \alpha\theta)$
length before heating $= l_0$
change in length $= l - l_0$
change in temp. $= \theta$

Question 3 (LON multiple completion)
The graph illustrates the relationship between the volume of a given mass of water and the temperature of the water.

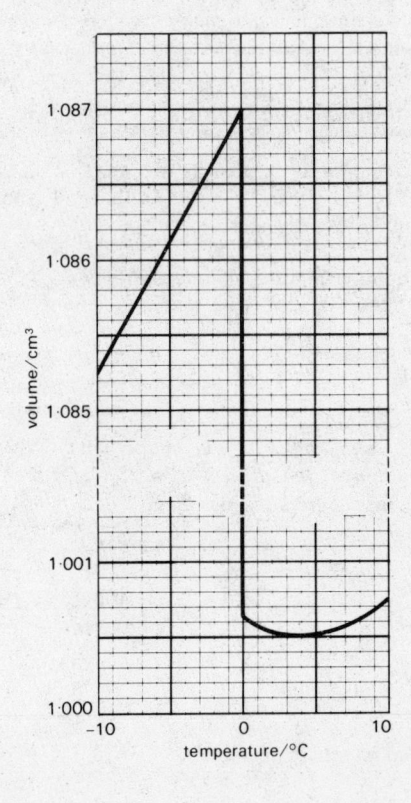

The graph shows that
1 *ice contracts when it melts*
2 *water has a maximum density at about 4°C*
3 *ice is less dense than water*

Answer: 1, 2 and 3
1 is common sense (think about burst pipes!).
2 can be seen from the graph: $\text{density} = \dfrac{\text{mass}}{\text{volume}}$, so its volume is least when its density is greatest.

Longer Questions

Question 1 (AEB)
(a) (i) State a formula which enables you to calculate the linear expansion of a substance and explain the meaning of any symbols used.
(ii) Sketch a graph to show how the volume of a fixed mass of water varies between 0°C and 10°C.
(iii) Sketch a graph to show how the volume of a fixed mass of gas varies between 0°C and 100°C if the pressure remains constant. *(9 marks)*
(b) Explain briefly how you would calibrate the 0°C mark on a mercury-in-glass thermometer. *(3 marks)*
(c) A mercury-in-glass thermometer with only the 0°C and 100°C markings on it was given to a student, and the student was asked to use it to estimate the temperature of a block of ice cream. Explain how the student could do this. *(7 marks)*
(d) The flask contains a liquid of boiling point 140°C. Initially when at room temperature the liquid level is at A as shown. When the flask is placed in hot water the liquid level first falls below A and then rises above A. Explain these observations. *(5 marks)*

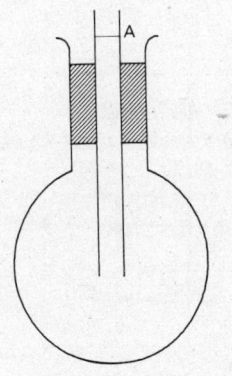

(e)

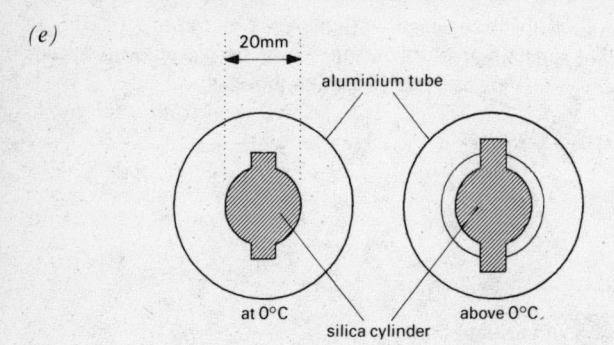

at 0°C — aluminium tube — silica cylinder — above 0°C

The diagram shows an aluminium tube containing a silica cylinder. The silica cylinder acts as a thermal tap to control the flow of liquid down the tube. At 0°C the cylinder has a diameter of 20 mm, there is an exact fit and no liquid flows. Calculate the size of the gap between cylinder and tube at 100°C. *(7 marks)*
(Linear expansivity of aluminium = 0·000026/K; linear expansivity of silica = 0·000008/K.)

Answer
(a) (i) $e = l_0 \alpha \theta$
e – expansion (or contraction)
l_0 – length at 0°C (or original length)
α – linear expansivity
θ – change in temp. from 0°C (or original temperature)

(ii) Graph of vol. of fixed mass of water v. temp.

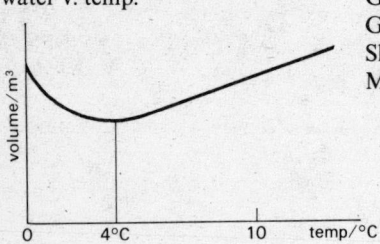

Comment
'State' = just write it down.
Then list symbols and explain each one.

'Sketch a graph'.
Give labelled axes with units.
Give title.
Show general shape.
Mark in any known points.

(iii) Graph of vol. of fixed mass of gas v. temp. for constant pressure

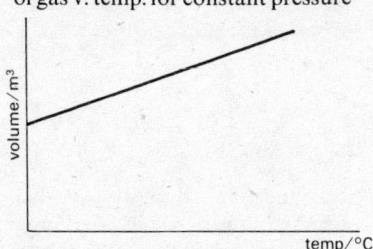

[Graph: volume/m³ vs temp/°C, straight line not passing through origin]

All the above, but notice that temp. is in °C, so the graph will *not* go through the origin.

(b) See answer to Question 1 (a), p. 82.

(c) Since the ice cream is likely to be below 0°C, the scale on the thermometer must be extended below the 0°C mark. There are a hundred divisions between the 0°C and the 100°C mark, so the length can be calculated in divisions. The distance of the mercury thread below the 0°C mark is measured, then translated into a number of divisions and so into the temperature below 0°C of ice cream.

Think about the practical aspect. Ice cream should be *cold*, so decide whether the mercury will be above or below 0°C.
Use known length to calibrate the scale.

(d) When placed in hot water (at a lower temperature than the boiling point of the liquid) the glass container expands before the heat is conducted through the glass (a poor conductor) to the liquid. The level therefore falls below A. When the heat reaches the liquid it expands and the level rises above A.

Liquids must be in containers, and you must remember that they expand as well as the liquid.

(e) Both the aluminium and the silica tap will expand when heated.
Silica: $l_0 = 20$ mm
$l_{100} = ?$ mm
$\alpha_{si} = 0 \cdot 000008$/K
$\theta = 100$ K
$l = l_0(1 + \alpha\theta)$
$= 20(1 + 0 \cdot 000008 \times 100)$
$= 20 \cdot 016$ mm

Consider silica and aluminium separately.
List information in question.

Quote formula.

Aluminium: The expansion of the hole in the aluminium is the same as the expansion of the disc which has been removed.

$l_0 = 20$ mm $\alpha_{Al} = 0.000026/K$
$l_{100} = ?$ mm $\theta = 100$ K
$l_{100} = l_0(1 + \alpha\theta)$
$\quad\quad = 20(1 + 0.000026 \times 100)$
$\quad\quad = 20.052$ mm

Size of gap $= \dfrac{d_2 - d_1}{2}$

$\quad\quad\quad\quad = \dfrac{20.052 - 20.016}{2}$

$\quad\quad\quad\quad = 0.018$ mm

Expansion of holes should always be thought of in terms of the expansion of the removed metal.

A diagram may clarify for you what the size of the gap is in relation to what you have already worked out. Don't forget *units* for answer.

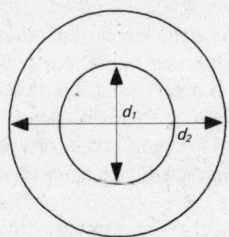

Question 2
An example of AEB's questions to test familiarity with laboratory work.
   You are instructed to determine by experiment the linear expansivity of a metal in the form of a rod or tube.
(a) Draw a labelled diagram of the apparatus you would use.
(b) Describe how you would perform the experiment, stating any precautions you would take to ensure an accurate result.
(c) List the quantities you would measure.
(d) State approximate sizes of these quantities.
(e) Show how you would use the quantities to calculate the linear expansivity.

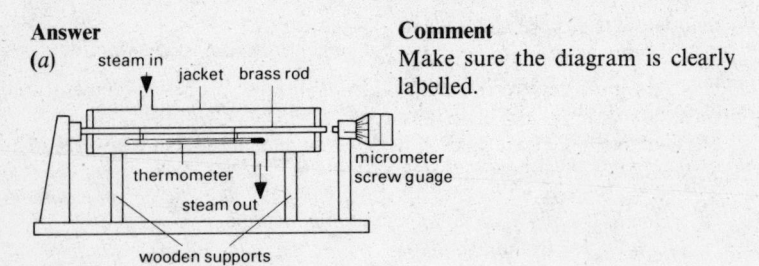

Answer
(a)

Comment
Make sure the diagram is clearly labelled.

(b) The length (l_0) of the rod is measured with a metre rule before it is placed in the steam jacket. Room temperature is also taken. The micrometer screw gauge is screwed up until it touches the rod, and its reading taken. It is then unscrewed. Steam is passed through the jacket for some minutes and its temperature noted. The micrometer screw gauge is readjusted to touch the rod and the new reading is taken. It is then unscrewed, readjusted after a few minutes and the reading checked.

Think about all the quantities you need to measure *before* you pass the steam.

N.B. don't forget precautions.

(c)/(d) Length of rod $l_0 = 50$ cm
Initial temp. of rod $\theta_1 = 17°C$
Final temp. of rod $\theta_2 = 100°C$
First micrometer reading m_1
  $= 4.50$ mm
Second micrometer reading m_2
  $= 3.85$ mm

Easier to do (c) and (d) together.

Don't forget: $m_1 < m_2$.
Give symbols to be used in part (e).

(e) $e = l_0 \times \alpha \times \theta$

$$\alpha = \frac{e}{l_0 \theta} = \frac{m_1 - m_2}{l_0(\theta_2 - \theta_1)}$$

Units are /K.

Expansion of Gases and the Gas Laws

Gas expansion can be caused by temperature *and* by pressure changes.

The **general gas law** $\dfrac{p_1 V_1}{T_1} = \dfrac{p_2 V_2}{T_2}$ should be known.

It is very important to remember that in all these problems temperature must be measured in Kelvin (absolute) ($T/K = \theta/°C + 273$).

Particular cases, **Boyle's law**, **Charles' law** and the **pressure law** need to be known for experimental verification.

Multiple Choice Questions

Question 1 (LON)
100 cm³ of dry air at a pressure of 1 atmosphere and temperature of 27°C are compressed to 5 atmospheres and heated to 77°C. The new volume is

A $\dfrac{3000}{7} \, cm^3$

B $\dfrac{350}{3} \, cm^3$

C $\dfrac{1540}{27} \, cm^3$

D $\dfrac{70}{3} \, cm^3$

E $\dfrac{120}{7} \, cm^3$

Answer: D
N.B. temp. in Kelvin.
$$p_1 = 1 \text{ atmos.} \quad p_2 = 5 \text{ atmos.}$$
$$T_1 = 27°C = 300 \text{ K}$$
$$T_2 = 77°C = 350 \text{ K}$$
$$V_1 = 100 \text{ cm}^3 \quad V_2 = ?$$

$$\frac{p_1 V_1}{T_1} = \frac{p_2 V_2}{T_2}$$

$$\frac{1 \times 100}{300} = \frac{5 \times V_2}{350}$$

$$V_2 = \frac{350 \times 100}{300 \times 5}$$

$$= \frac{70}{3} \, cm^3$$

(Immediately discard **C**, since temperature has not been converted to Kelvin.)

Question 2 (AEB)
The absolute temperature of a fixed mass of gas was doubled and its volume was halved. If the original pressure was p the final pressure would be

A $\tfrac{1}{4}p$
B $\tfrac{1}{2}p$
C   p
D   2p
E   4p

Answer: E

$$\frac{p_1 V_1}{T_1} = \frac{p_2 V_2}{T_2}$$

$$\frac{p \times V}{T} = \frac{p_2 \times \tfrac{1}{2}V}{2T}$$

$$p_2 = 4p$$

Heat 97

Question 3 (AEB)

Which one of these graphs correctly represents the variation of pressure with absolute temperature for a fixed mass of gas at constant volume?

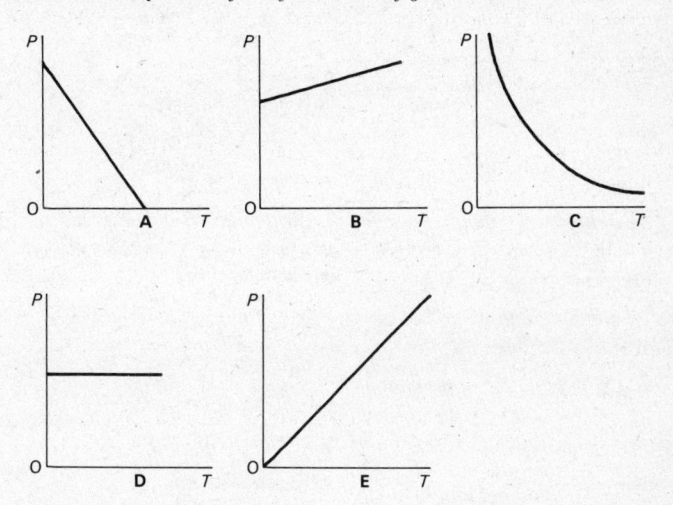

Answer: E
The important point to notice is *'absolute temperature'*; you therefore expect the graph to go through the origin.

Longer Questions

Question 1 (AEB)

(a) When defining Boyle's law:

 (i) which two physical quantities are related to each other?
 (ii) how are they related?
 (iii) which physical quantities remain constant? (6 marks)

(b) The diagrams overleaf show the same uniform-bore glass tube containing dry air sealed by a thread of mercury in two positions.

98 *Passnotes:* **Physics**

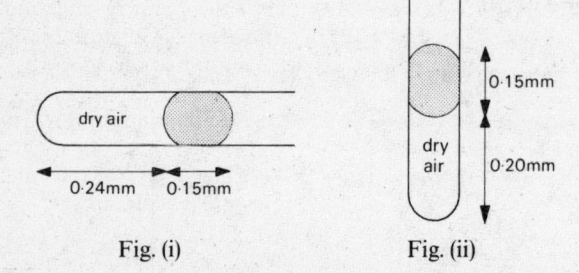

Fig. (i)

Fig. (ii)

(i) write down an expression for pressure on the trapped air in Fig (i).
(ii) Write down an expression for pressure on the trapped air in Fig. (ii).
(iii) Hence calculate the atmospheric pressure. (9 marks)

(c) If the temperature of the air in Fig. (i) were slowly increased, what effect would this have on:

(i) the length of the air column?
(ii) the molecules in the air column? (4 marks)
(Density of mercury = 13 600 kg/m³; g = 10 m/s².)

Answer

(a) (i) Pressure and volume.
(ii) Pressure × volume
= constant.

(iii) Temperature and mass of gas.
(b) (i) Pressure on trapped air = atmospheric pressure p.
Length of tube $\propto$ volume of air trapped, as area of cross section is constant.
$p \times 0.24 \times 10^{-3}$ = constant
(ii) In this situation:
pressure = p + pressure due to mercury
= $p + h\rho g$
= $p + 0.15 \times 10^{-3} \times 13600 \times 10$
= $p + 20.4$
$(p + 20.4) \times 0.20 \times 10^{-3}$ = constant

Comment

Boyle's law: For a fixed mass of gas at constant temperature:

$$p_1 V_1 = p_2 V_2$$

N.B. in (iii), note plural and be sure you think of more than one.
Explain why you can take lengths as in diagram to be proportional to volume.

Convert all units to SI, since density of mercury and g are given in these.

Pressure in a liquid = $h\rho g$: see p. 61.

Heat 99

(iii) $p \times 0.24 \times 10^{-3} = (p + 20.4) \times 0.20 \times 10^{-3}$

Since there are two situations, this should make you expect two simultaneous equations to solve.

$p \times 1.2 = p + 20.4$
$0.2p = 20.4$
$p = 102 \text{ N/m}^2$

Divide both sides by 0.2×10^{-3}.

Be careful to use SI units for pressure in your answer.

(c) (i) When the temperature is increased in the first situation we can assume that the atmospheric pressure remains constant, so the volume of air will expand (as $V \propto T$) and the length of trapped air will increase.

$T_1 > T_2$ and $\dfrac{p_1 V_1}{T_1} = \dfrac{p_2 V_2}{T_2}$

Since pressure is constant, V must increase.

(ii) According to the *kinetic theory*, the average velocity of molecules depends on their temperature. The increase in temperature therefore means that the molecules of dry air move faster.

'Molecules' in the question should make you think of the kinetic theory.

Question 2 (L O N part question)
Describe how you would investigate the variation of volume with temperature of a fixed mass of dry air at constant pressure. Explain why you think the pressure is kept constant in your experiment. (8 marks)

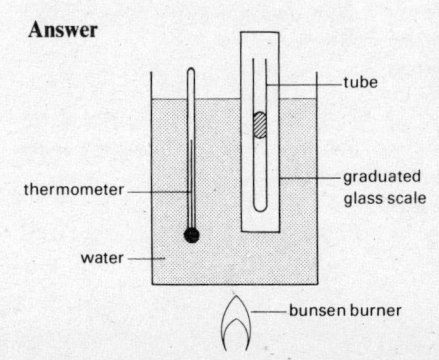

Answer

Comment
Make sure all the dry air is under the water. Explain how to find (a) temperature and (b) volume measurements. You cannot measure volume itself, so explain how you deal with this problem.
Remember: length × area of cross-section = volume.

A short length of mercury is introduced into a glass capillary tube so that dry air is trapped between it and the closed end of the capillary tube, as shown in the diagram. This apparatus is then attached to a graduated scale and placed in a beaker of water. The temperature of the dry air is the same as that of the water, so that is measured with a mercury-in-glass thermometer.

The bottom of the dry-air column is aligned with the zero mark on the graduated scale, and the length of the column is read off the scale at various temperatures. The area of cross-section of the tube is considered to be uniform, so the length of the column can be taken as proportional to the volume of dry air. The water should be stored so that the water and air temperatures stay the same.

Always give experimental details if possible.

A graph of length of air column versus temperature should be drawn. This should be a straight line, but it will not pass through the origin unless the temperature is measured in Kelvin.

Say what you expect the graph to look like.

The pressure on the gas is made up of both atmospheric pressure (assumed to be constant through the experiment) and that due to the mercury. This is equal to the height of the mercury (which stays the same in the experiment) multiplied by the density of mercury and by the acceleration due to gravity, both of which should be constant.

Remember, pressure due to mercury $= h\rho g$ (see p. 61).

Heat 101

Question 3 (LON)

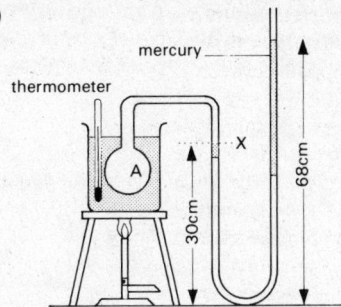

The diagram shows an apparatus which can be used to investigate how the pressure of a fixed mass of air at a constant volume trapped in the bulb A varies with temperature.

(a) (i) How would you ensure that all the air trapped in the bulb A was at the temperature recorded by the thermometer? *(2 marks)*

(ii) Why, when taking readings of the pressure, is it necessary to ensure that the mercury level coincides each time with the mark X? *(2 marks)*

(iii) Using the values given in the diagram, calculate the total pressure of the air trapped in the bulb A, given that the height of a mercury barometer in the laboratory is 76 cm. (The pressure of 76 cm of mercury is equivalent to 1×10^5 Pa.) *(3 marks)*

(iv) Sketch a graph of the results that would be obtained from such an experiment. What conclusion could be drawn from the graph? What do you understand by absolute zero of temperature? *(6 marks)*

(v) Explain briefly how the kinetic theory of gases accounts for the results obtained in the above experiment. *(4 marks)*

(b) A bottle is corked when the air inside is at $20°C$ and the pressure is $1·0 \times 10^5$ Pa. If the cork blows out when the pressure is $3·0 \times 10^5$ Pa, calculate the temperature to which the bottle must be heated for this to happen. (Assume that the bottle does not expand.) *(3 marks)*

Answer

(*a*) (i) The bulb must be submerged under the water and should be left at the same temperature for some time.

(ii) The experiment is for a constant volume of gas, so to ensure this the mercury is moved back to X each time the pressure is read.

Comment

Only 2 marks, so not much detail needed.

(iii) Pressure on A = atmospheric pressure + pressure due to difference in mercury levels
= 76 + 38 cm of mercury
= 114 cm of Hg
(= $1 \cdot 5 \times 10^5$ Pa)

(iv)
Graph of pressure v. temperature for a fixed mass of gas at constant volume

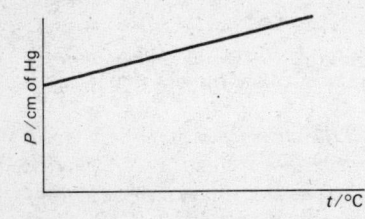

Atmospheric pressure is given in cm of mercury, so your answer can be as well.

The graph should be of quantities measured, so t will be in °C and the graph will not go through origin.

N.B. label axes of graph with quantity and unit, and give it a title.

[Graph: P/cm of Hg vs t/°C, showing a line with positive slope not passing through origin]

This graph shows pressure ∝ temp. (°C) + constant.
If the graph were extrapolated backwards, it would cross the x-axis at −273°C, the **absolute zero** of temperature.

Conclusion from graph.

Give value of *absolute zero* in °C, too.

(v) See answers to Question 1, p. 78, and Question 2, p. 79.

(b) $p_1 = 1 \cdot 0 \times 10^5$ Pa $T_1 = 20°C$
                                              $= 293$ K
$p_2 = 3 \cdot 0 \times 10^5$ Pa $T_2 = ?$

Remember to convert °C to K.
List quantities given in question, then quote formula.

$$\frac{p_1 V_1}{T_1} = \frac{p_2 V_2}{T_2}$$

Volume is constant,

$$\therefore \frac{1 \cdot 0 \times 10^5}{293} = \frac{3 \cdot 0 \times 10^5}{T_2}$$

$T_2 = 879$ K
    $= 606°C$

Since first temperature was given in °C, you should do the same in your answer.

Heat 103

Specific Heat Capacity

Specific Heat Capacity (S.H.C.) is the quantity of energy (heat) required to raise the temperature of 1 kg of a substance by 1°C.
Heat energy (J) = S.H.C. (J/kgK) × mass (kg) × temperature change (K)
Heat capacity (J/K) = mass (kg) × S.H.C. (J/kgK)
Methods of measuring S.H.C. by electrical heating for solids and liquids.

Multiple Choice Questions

Question 1 (AEB)
5632 J of heat energy raise the temperature of 0·4 kg of aluminium from 20°C to 36°C. The specific heat capacity of aluminium in J/kgK is given by

A $5632 \times 0.4 \times 16$

B $\dfrac{5632}{0.4 \times 16}$

C $\dfrac{5632 \times 16}{0.4}$

D $\dfrac{5632 \times 0.4}{16}$

E $\dfrac{0.4 \times 16}{5632}$

Answer: B
From equation:

Energy = S.H.C. × mass × change in temp.

5632 (J) = S.H.C. × 0.4 (kg) × 16°(C)

S.H.C. = $\dfrac{5632}{0.4 \times 16}$

Question 2
An example of London's grouped questions dealing with a practical situation.

A thin plastic container of negligible heat capacity holds a mass of liquid to which a quantity of energy is added using an immersion heater.

(i) If the mass of liquid is 5·0 kg and its specific heat capacity is 2000 J/kgK, a temperature rise of 10 K will require

A 100 000 J
B 10 000 J
C 4000 J
D 1000 J
E 400 J

Answer: A
Energy = S.H.C. × mass × change in temp.
= 2000 × 5·0 × 10
= 100 000 J

(ii) The same amount of energy is now supplied to a smaller mass of the same liquid. If the temperature rise is now 12·5 K the mass of the liquid is

A   2·0 kg
B   2·5 kg
C   3·0 kg
D   4·0 kg
E   4·5 kg

Answer: D
Energy = S.H.C. × mass × change in temp.
$100000 = 2000 \times m \times 12\cdot 5$
$m = 4\cdot 0$ kg
(Same liquid, so same S.H.C.)

(iii) The container is emptied and 5·0 kg of another liquid is poured into it. If the temperature rise is now 5 K and the heat energy supplied is the same as before, then the specific heat capacity of the liquid is

A   1000 J/kgK
B   2000 J/kgK
C   2500 J/kgK
D   4000 J/kgK
E   25000 J/kgK

Answer: D
Energy = S.H.C. × mass × change in temp.
$100000 = $ S.H.C. $\times 5\cdot 0 \times 5$
S.H.C. = 4000 J/kgK
N.B. all questions rely on the same formula and on getting the first answer right.

Longer Questions

Question 1 (OXF part question)
If the power of a heater is 1250 W, how long will it take to raise the temperature of 1·5 kg of water from 20°C to 50°C? Take the specific heat capacity of water to be 4200 J/kgK.

Answer
Energy = power × time
Energy = mass × S.HC × change in temperature
= 1·5 (kg) × 4200 (J/kgK) × 30 (K)
= 189000 J
∴ 189000 (J) = 1250 (W) × time(s)
time = 151·2 s

Comment
Quote necessary formulae.

Remember: for temperature change, °C is the same as K.

You can leave the answer in seconds.

Question 2 (LON)

(a) Describe an experiment you would perform to find the S.H.C. of a liquid. State the precautions you would take to obtain an accurate result, and show how you could calculate the result. *(10 marks)*

(b) A saucepan of mass 0·75 kg containing 0·50 kg of water is placed on a gas burner. The initial temperature of the water is 20°C. It takes 5 minutes before the water starts to boil. Find the rate at which the heat is supplied to the water by the burner. *(7 marks)*
(S.H.K. of water = 4000 J/kgK. S.H.C. of the material of the saucepan = 600 J/kgK.)

(c) It is found to take less time to boil water and cook vegetables in a saucepan with a lid than in a similar saucepan without a lid. Explain why this is so. *(3 marks)*

Answer
(a)

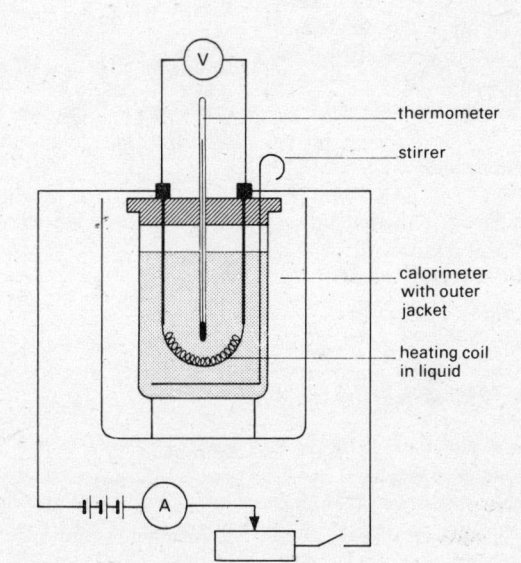

labels: V, thermometer, stirrer, calorimeter with outer jacket, heating coil in liquid, A

The calorimeter is first weighed empty and then three-quarters full of liquid. The initial temperature of the liquid is taken and the current switched on simultaneously with the timer. The voltmeter reading is taken and a steady

Comment
Answer plan
(1) Diagram of apparatus.
(2) Method.
(3) Precautions.
(4) Calculation of results.
Think about what you will need to

current maintained for about 5 minutes, the liquid being stirred continuously. At the end of 5 minutes the current is switched off and the final steady temperature is taken.

The calorimeter is lagged to prevent as much heat loss to the surroundings as possible, and is well polished. The experiment should be tested first to find a suitable current that gives a temperature rise of about 10°C in 5 minutes. If the liquid is cooled 5°C below room temperature and heated to 5°C above room temperature, heat losses will be reduced.

Mass of calorimeter + stirrer = m_1 kg
Mass of calorimeter + stirrer + liquid = m_2 kg
∴ mass of liquid = $m_2 - m_1$ kg
Initial temp. of liquid = θ_1 °C
Final temp. of liquid = θ_2 °C
Rise in temp. for liquid (and calorimeter) = $\theta_2 - \theta_1$ °C
Current = I A
P.d. across heater coil = V V
Time = t s
S.H.C. of calorimeter = c J/kgK

Energy = power × time
Energy from heater = VIt J: this supplies energy to liquid and calorimeter.
Energy = S.H.C. × mass × temp. change
For calorimeter, energy = $c \times m_1 \times (\theta_2 - \theta_1)$ J
For liquid, energy = S.H.C. × $(m_2 - m_1) \times (\theta_2 - \theta_1)$
∴ $VIt = [c \times m_1 \times (\theta_2 - \theta_1)] + [\text{S.H.C.} \times (m_2 - m_1) \times (\theta_2 - \theta_1)]$
Hence S.H.C.

know to calculate S.H.C., and check you measure them all.
Energy = power × time
= $V \times I \times$ time (see p. 52).
Energy = S.H.C. × mass × change in temp.
Heat loss is bound to be the main problem, so think of all possible precautions.

Give letters to quantities measured rather than guessing numbers.

Don't forget that the liquid container takes in heat, too.

Don't bother to work out final equation. 'Hence' is a *most* useful word.

Heat 107

(b) Boiling point of water = 100°C
∴ temperature change = 100 − 20
= 80°C

Heat energy = S.H.C. × mass × change in temp.

Saucepan:
$E_1 = 600 \, (J/kgK) \times 0.75 \, (kg) \times 80 \, (°C)$
$= 36000 \, J$

Water:
$E_2 = 4000 \, (J/kgK) \times 0.50 \, (kg) \times 80 \, (°C)$
$= 160000 \, J$

Total energy supplied = $E_1 + E_2$
= 196000 J

Rate at which energy is supplied

$$= \frac{\text{energy}}{\text{time}}$$

$$= \frac{196000 \, (J)}{5 \times 60 \, (s)}$$

$$= 653\tfrac{1}{3} \, J/s$$

(c) When the lid is on the saucepan the water vapour is kept in. Since it is at a higher temperature than the liquid the overall temperature inside the saucepan will rise, and heat loss by evaporation will also be reduced, so it will take less time to boil the water than with the lid off.

Remember, heat to *both* liquid and saucepan, and temperature change will be the same for both.

N.B. time in *seconds*.
Always use SI units.

Here, unit can be J/s or W.
The only change will be the steam is kept in – so think what difference that will make.

Change of State and Specific Latent Heat

Fusion, evaporation, vapour pressure, saturated vapour pressure, boiling (including effects of pressure and impurities).
Specific latent heats of fusion and vaporization and experimental methods to find these.
Specific latent heat (S.L.H.) (J/kg) × mass (kg) = energy (J)
Cooling by evaporation, refrigeration.
Much of this work is often dealt with in terms of the kinetic theory; see also 'Heat as a Form of Energy. The Kinetic Theory', pp. 77–80.

Multiple Choice Questions

Question 1 (A E B)
The freezing chamber of a refrigerator is positioned

A near the top as cold air is less dense than warm air
B near the top as cold air is more dense than warm air
C in the middle as hot air rises and cold air falls
D near the bottom as cold air is less dense than warm air
E near the bottom as cold air is more dense than warm air

Answer: B
Common experience suggests **A** or **B**. As volume of gas ∝ temperature, and density ∝ $\frac{1}{\text{volume}}$, hot air is less dense than cold air.

Question 2 (A E B)
If the specific latent heat of steam at $100°C$ is $2\cdot26 \times 10^6$ J/kg, the heat in J required to evaporate 2 g of water at $100°C$ is

A $2\cdot00 \times 10^2$
B $1\cdot13 \times 10^3$
C $4\cdot52 \times 10^3$
D $1\cdot13 \times 10^6$
E $4\cdot52 \times 10^6$

Answer: C
N.B. look out for units.
$2 \text{ g} = 2 \times 10^{-3}$ kg
Energy = mass × S.L.H.
$= 2 \times 10^{-3} \times 2\cdot26 \times 10^6$ J
$= 4\cdot52 \times 10^3$ J

Question 3 (A E B multiple completion)
While a given mass of ice is changing from the solid state to the liquid state there is no change in

1 mass
2 temperature
3 volume

Answer 1 and 2
(N.B. think of burst pipes!)

Question 4 (A E B)
When salt is added to an icy road the ice melts because

A the salt is warmer than ice
B heat is given out as salt dissolves in water
C ice crystals cannot exist in the presence of salt crystals
D a solution of salt in water is less viscous than pure water
E a solution of salt in water has a lower freezing point than pure water

Answer: E
C is unlikely and D has little to do with melting.

Longer Questions

Question 1 (A E B)
(a) Define and name the units of
  (i) specific heat capacity, and
  (ii) specific latent heat.   *(6 marks)*

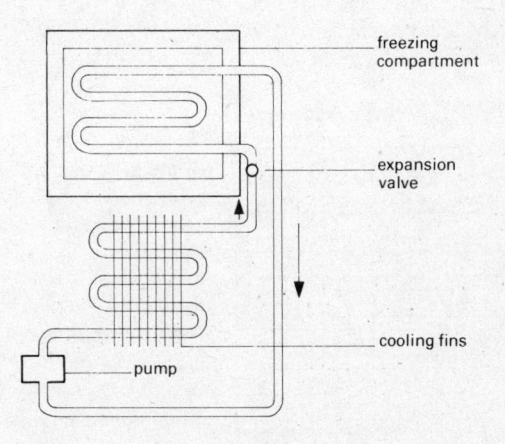

(b) The diagram shows a simple refrigerator, and the arrows indicate the direction in which the refrigerant flows. Explain what is happening
  (i) in the tubes in the freezing compartment, and
  (ii) in the tubes connected to the cooling fins
  For each location, name the state of the refrigerant.   *(6 marks)*

Answer
(a) **Specific heat capacity** is the amount of energy required to change the temperature of 1 kg of a substance by 1°K.   Unit: J/kgK

Specific latent heat is the amount of energy required to change 1 kg of a substance from one state to another without change of temperature.   Unit: J/kg.

(b) (i) In the freezing compartment the refrigerant evaporates as the expansion valve reduces the pressure on it. The S.L.H. comes from the refrigerant's own internal energy, so it cools down. The refrigerant is a *gas* here.

(ii) The pump compresses the gas so that it liquefies and its S.L.H. is given out; this needs to be removed by the cooling fins. The refrigerant is a *liquid* here.

Comment
Definitions you need to know.

Only 6 marks, so there is no need to go into a lot of detail.

Question 2 (LON part question)

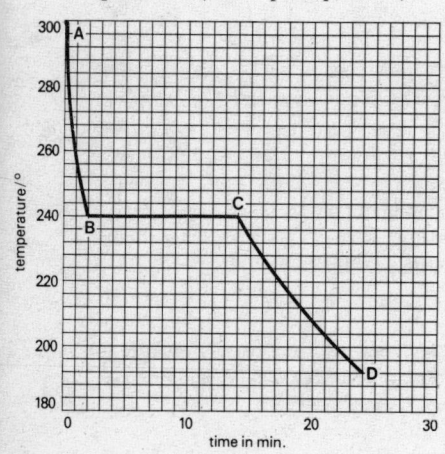

The graph shows the variation of temperature with time for a pure metal cooling from 300°C. In what state is the metal in stage
(a) AB
(b) BC
(c) CD   *(3 marks)*
If the average rate of heat loss during stage BC is 120 J/min and the mass of metal is 80 g, what is the specific latent heat of fusion of the metal?   *(4 marks)*

Heat 111

Answer
(a) Molten.
(b) Both molten and solid, as it changes state.
(c) Solid.

Energy = mass × S.L.H.
Change of state occurs for 12 min
∴ energy = 120 (J/min) × 12 (min)
= 1440 J
1440 (J) = 0·08 (kg) × L (J/kg)
L = 18 000 J/kg

Comment
Obviously there is only one mark for each question, so one word will do.

Read off the graph.

Remember to change mass to *kg*.

Question 3 (AEB)
(a) Name two factors which affect the boiling point of water, and in each case state how the boiling point is affected. (2 marks)
(b) Distinguish between evaporation and boiling. (4 marks)

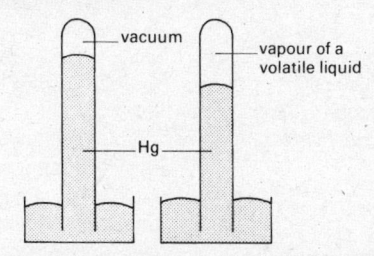

(c) The diagrams show a glass tube before and after a small amount of a volatile liquid has been introduced into the space above the mercury. Explain why the mercury in the right-hand tube is lower than that in the left-hand tube. (2 marks)

Answer
(a) Impurities in the water. Pressure on the water.
(b) Evaporation occurs at any temperature, and is the loss of faster-moving molecules from liquid to gaseous state. Boiling occurs at a fixed temperature when all the molecules have enough energy to escape.

Comment
Only 2 marks, so just *name* them; don't explain.

The important point is temperature difference.

(c) The molecules of the volatile liquid's vapour have velocity, and thereby produce a pressure as they collide with the mercury's surface which acts in the opposite direction to atmospheric pressure; so the barometer is lower.

Obviously, the pressure differs because the barometer is lower, so account for that.

General Questions

Longer and more structured questions often test several aspects of the syllabus at once.

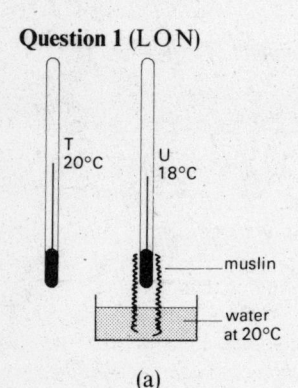

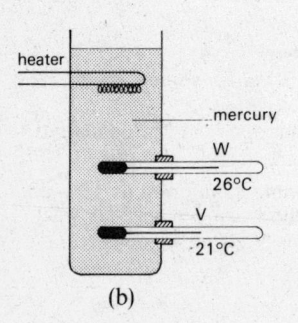

Question 1 (LON)

The diagrams illustrate three situations, (a), (b) and (c), involving thermometers. In each situation the thermometers, which you may assume to be accurate and not subject to error, indicate different temperatures.

(a) (i) Using the kinetic-molecular theory of matter, explain why the reading of thermometer U is less than that of thermometer T when they are placed side by side in the same room. (5 marks)

(ii) Name the instrument which uses this arrangement and state its practical use. (2 marks)

(b) Why is the reading of thermometer W greater than that of thermometer V? (3 marks)

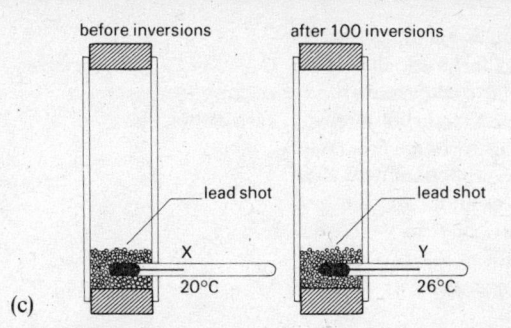

before inversions   after 100 inversions

lead shot — X — 20°C

lead shot — Y — 26°C

(c)

(c) (i) By describing the energy involved as the lead shot drops from the top to the bottom of the tube, explain why the reading of thermometer Y is greater than that of thermometer X. *(4 marks)*

(ii) Calculate the specific heat capacity of the lead shot if the distance fallen on each inversion is 1·0 m. *(4 marks)*

(iii) If the mass of the lead shot is increased, it is found that the rise in temperature of the lead shot after 100 inversions is still 6 K. Account for this. *(2 marks)*

Answer

(a) (i) The kinetic theory states that the average velocity of molecules depends on their temperature. Since the molecules of a gas move faster and are more spread out than those of a liquid, gas molecules have a higher energy. The muslin round the thermometer is saturated with water, some of which evaporates. The faster moving molecules escape, leaving behind those with a lower average velocity and so at a lower temperature.

(ii) The wet and dry hygrometer uses this arrangement to measure the relative humidity of the air.

(b) The heat from the heater moves through the mercury by *conduction*, since the molecules of mercury are closely packed and pass the

Comment

Answer plan

(1) State kinetic theory.

(2) Consider muslin and what its importance is. Give answer in terms of molecules.
(N.B. examiners stated that they gave no marks for 'evaporation requires latent heat'.)

Only 2 marks – one for name and one for use.

N.B. liquid is *mercury*, so heat transfer is likely to be conduction.

heat by vibrations of molecules. As *W* is nearer the heater than *V*, it will receive more heat than *V*.

(*c*) (i) When the lead shot is at the top of the tube it gains kinetic energy. The experimenter then turns the tube and gives the lead shot more energy. After 100 inversions the energy gained by the lead shot is shown as a rise in temperature.

Remember to answer in terms of energy.

(ii) Potential energy
$$= mgh$$
$$= m \times 10 \times 1\cdot 0 \text{ J}$$
In 100 inversions energy gained
$$= m \times 10 \times 1\cdot 0 \times 100 \text{ J}$$
Energy = mass × S.H.C.
× temp. change
$$= m \times c \times 6$$
$m \times 10 \times 1\cdot 0 \times 100 = m \times c \times 6$

$$\frac{1000}{6} = c$$

$$c = 166\cdot 7 \text{ J/kgK}$$

Quote formula used.
N.B. *g*'s value will often be given at the front of the paper.
Remember: more than one inversion.

N.B. *units* for answer.

(iii) In calculating the temperature rise the same formulae as above are used, and the mass cancelled out as shown above; so change in mass will not affect change in temperature.

Only 2 marks, but be sure your explanation is clear.

Question 2 (AEB)

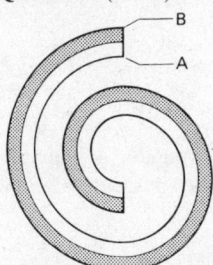

(a) The diagram shows a bimetallic strip wound into a flat spiral. Metal A has a higher expansivity than metal B. Describe and explain what happens when the strip is heated.
(3 marks)

(b) When constructing a thermometer for normal laboratory use the bulb is made of thin glass, the bore of the tube is narrow, and mercury is used as the thermometric liquid. Explain why:
   (i) the bulb is of thin glass,
   (ii) the bore is narrow, and
   (iii) mercury is chosen. *(5 marks)*

(c) Draw a labelled diagram of a clinical thermometer and state two ways in which it differs from a normal laboratory thermometer. *(7 marks)*

(d) Before starting a long journey, a motorist checked his tyre pressures and found them to be 3×10^5 Pa. At the end of the journey the pressures were found to be $3 \cdot 3 \times 10^5$ Pa. The temperature of the tyres and contained air at the start of the journey was $17°$ C. Assuming the volume of the tyres remains constant, determine the temperature of the air in the tyres at the end of the journey. *(6 marks)*

Answer

(a) When the strip is heated it unwinds, since A expands more than B for the same temperature change.

(b) (i) Glass is a poor conductor of heat; it is made thin so that the heat reaches the mercury quickly.

(ii) The bore is narrow, so small temperature changes produce fairly large changes in the mercury level.

(iii) Mercury is chosen as it is easy to see, and its freezing and boiling points are outside the ordinary range of laboratory temperatures.

Comment

First describe what happens and then explain it. They have the same temperature change, so think about which expands more.

5 marks for three answers, so they can be fairly brief.

(c)

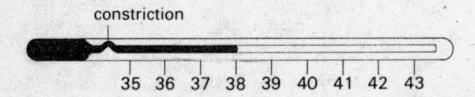

(1) A constriction in the bore means that the mercury stays in the bore when the temperature changes, and can be read at leisure.

(2) The range of the thermometer is restricted to a few degrees on either side of normal body temperature.

Two ways asked for, so number them and make sure your diagram shows both.

(d) $\dfrac{p_1 V_1}{T_1} = \dfrac{p_2 V_2}{T_2}$ for a fixed mass of gas.
V is constant.
$p_1 = 3 \times 10^5$ Pa
$p_2 = 3 \cdot 3 \times 10^5$ Pa
$T_1 = 17°C = 290$ K
$T_2 = ?$

$$\frac{3 \times 10^5}{290} = \frac{3 \cdot 3 \times 10^5}{T_2}$$

$$T_2 = \frac{3 \cdot 3 \times 10^5 \times 290}{3 \times 10^5}$$

$$= 319 \text{ K}$$

Final temperature = 46°C

Obviously a gas law question, so
(1) quote formula, and
(2) remember to convert temperature to Kelvin.

Give final answer in °C to match question.

Section 5: Waves, Sound and Light

Vibrations and Waves

Free and forced **vibrations**.
Resonance (which occurs when a particular body or system is set in oscillation at its own natural frequency, as a result of impulses received from some other system which is vibrating with the same frequency). (See also Section 3, which includes questions on vibrating bodies such as pendulums, and 'Sound', pp. 123–9.)

Amplitude: the maximum displacement of a particle from its rest position.
Period (T): the time taken for one oscillation (unit: second).
Frequency (f): the number of oscillations per second (unit: hertz)
$$T = \frac{1}{f}.$$
Vibrating systems as sources of **waves**.
Transverse (vibrations at right angles to wave direction) and **longitudinal** (vibrations along the same direction as wave direction) **waves**.
Velocity of a wave and its dependence on the medium through which the wave travels.
Wavelength(λ): the distance between two successive particles which are at exactly the same point in their paths and are moving in the same direction (i.e. are in phase).
The wave equation: $v = f\lambda$.
Properties of water waves as shown in the ripple tank: **reflection, refraction, diffraction, interference**.
[Sound waves will be studied under 'Sound'.]

Multiple Choice Questions

Question 1 (LON matching pairs question)
The following terms are used in the study of waves

A amplitude
B diffraction
C frequency
D resonance
E reflection

Which of these

(i) allows waves to spread outside apertures and round corners?

Answer: B
You need to know what all the words in this list mean, as they often appear in multiple choice questions.

(ii) is responsible for the production of echoes?

Answer: E
An echo is just sound bouncing off a hard substance.

(iii) is measured as a distance?

Answer: A
B, D and E are wave properties and are not measured.

Question 2 (A E B)

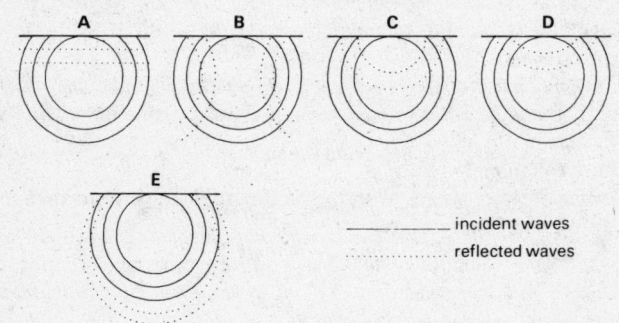

——— incident waves
·········· reflected waves

Which one of the above diagrams best illustrates the reflection of a wavefront by a plane reflecting surface in a ripple tank?

Waves, Sound and Light 119

Answer: D
The waves in **C** are much too sharply curved. If you imagine 'flipping back' the reflected rays of **D** across the barrier, you can see they would complete the circles: for no other case would this be true.

Question 3 (A E B)
A vibrator sends 6 ripples per second across a water tank. The ripples are observed to be 3 cm apart. The velocity in cm/s of the ripples is

A $\frac{1}{2}$
B *2*
C *9*
D *12*
E *18*

Answer: E
Here $f = 6$ hertz (Hz) (ripples/s)
$\lambda = 3$ cm
$v = f\lambda$
$v = 6 \text{ (Hz)} \times 3 \text{ (cm)}$
$= 18$ cm/s

Question 4 (L O N)
The basic difference between transverse and longitudinal mechanical waves is

A amplitude
B direction of vibration
C frequency
D medium through which they travel
E wavelength

Answer: B
You *must* know this difference. Any of the other distractors might be true for particular waves, but **B** is always true.

Question 5 (O X F)
If two waves interfere at a point so that at all times one exactly cancels the other, the two must have
A the same amplitude, different frequency, different phase
B the same amplitude, the same frequency, different phase
C different amplitude, the same frequency, different phase
D different amplitude, different frequency, the same phase
E the same amplitude, different frequency, the same phase

Answer: B
To cancel out, *amplitude* and *frequency* must be the same, but the waves must be in antiphase (180° out of phase).

Longer Questions

Question 1
Draw labelled diagrams showing water waves as seen in a ripple tank to illustrate (a) the reflection of circular waves by a plane surface, (b) the reflection of plane (straight) waves by a concave surface, (c) the refraction of water waves as they move to shallower water. (12 marks)

Answer   **Comment**

(a)

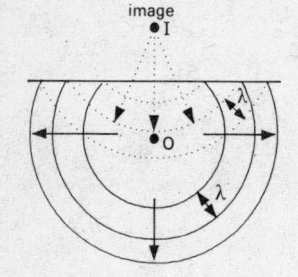

——— incident waves

······· reflected waves

λ is unchanged

I to barrier = O to barrier

You need to learn ripple tank diagrams.

Always show clearly:
(a) *incident waves* and direction,
(b) *reflected* or *refracted waves* and direction,
(c) *wavelengths* of (a) and (b),
(d) continuity of waves at boundaries or barriers.

(b)

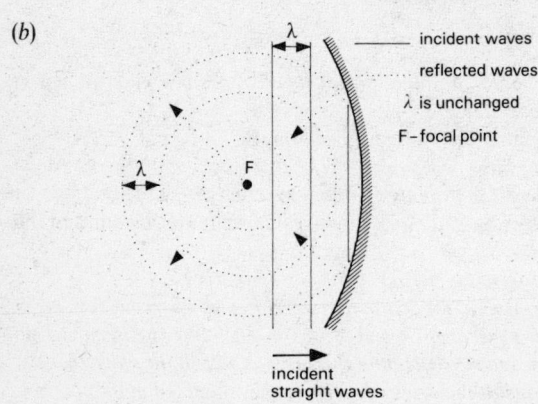

——— incident waves

······· reflected waves

λ is unchanged

F – focal point

incident straight waves

Waves, Sound and Light

(c)

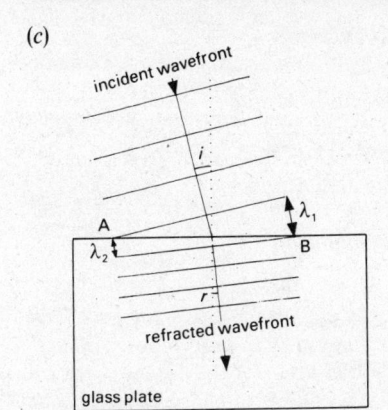

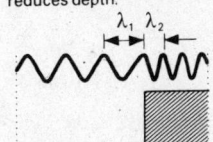

Waves travel more slowly in shallow water (same frequency, shorter wavelength).

A glass plate is put in the ripple tank, so one section of water is shallower than the rest.
The velocity and wavelength of the refracted waves are less than those of the incident waves.

Section: glass plate reduces depth.

Both velocity and wavelengths change in shallower water.
You can not only show change of wavelength, *but* also show the change in direction this produces.

N.B. the source hasn't changed, so the frequency isn't altered.

Question 2 (AEB part question)
The diagram shows a wave produced in a rope.

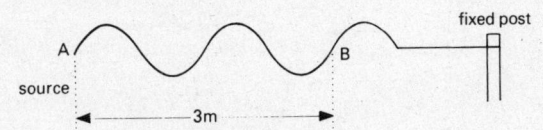

(i) What type of wave is produced?
(ii) How is this motion produced in the rope?
(iii) Copy the diagram and mark on your copy the wavelength and the amplitude of the wave.
(iv) What is meant by the period of the wave motion?
(v) How is the period of the wave motion related to its frequency?
(vi) If the distance between A and B is 3 m and the rope is moved up and down 4 times per second, calculate the speed at which the wave travels.
(vii) What happens to the wave when it reaches the fixed point?

Answer

(i) A transverse wave

(ii) The source is moved up and down at right angles to the line AB.

(iii)

[Diagram: wave between points A and B, with amplitude 'a' marked from centre to peak, wavelength λ marked between peaks, and a post at right.]

amplitude of wave — wavelength

(iv) The **period** is the time for a wave particle to make one complete oscillation (or the time for a cycle of the wave to pass a fixed point).

(v) Since **frequency** is the no. of cycles/s

$$\text{frequency} = \frac{1}{\text{period}}$$

(vi) From diagram:
 AB = 2 wavelengths
 ∴ λ = 1 m
 f = 4 Hz
 $v = f \times \lambda$
 v = 4(Hz) × 1(m)
  = 6 m/s

(vii) When the wave reaches the post it is reflected with a 180° phase change.

[Diagram: incident wave (solid) travelling right toward post, reflected wave (dotted) travelling left.]

incident wave
reflected wave

Comment

N.B. vibrations are at a right angle to motion, so are *transverse*.

If you read the question through, part (vi) helps with this.

Copy diagram and mark distances clearly.

N.B *amplitude* is from max. displacement to central position.
Wavelength is the distance between two points in phase; could also be peak to peak or trough to trough.

Important definition.

Important definition.

$\left(\text{Or period} = \dfrac{1}{\text{frequency}}\right)$

The hertz (Hz) unit is the same as /s or s^{-1}.
Quote formula and substitute.
Units!

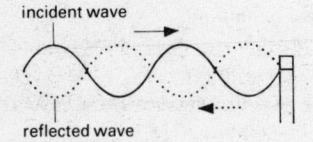

A diagram, no matter how rough, will help here.

Question 3 (LON)

The diagrams below show waves in a ripple tank approaching

(i) *a narrow gap in a barrier, and* (ii) *a wide gap in a barrier.*

Copy the diagrams and show the subsequent appearance of the waves.

Answer

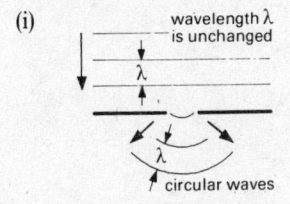

(i)

(ii)

Your diagrams should show clearly that (i) is *diffraction*, i.e. circular waves are formed, and that in (ii) there is only slight diffraction at the edges of the waves.

Sound

Production of sound by vibrating objects.
Transmission of sound – need for a material medium.
Reflection of sound: echoes.
Loudness of sound depending on the **amplitude** of the wave.
Pitch of sound depending on the **frequency** of the wave.
Determination of **velocity of sound** in free air.
Standing waves; nodes (positions of minimum vibration) and **antinodes** (positions of maximum vibration).
Vibrating strings and air columns, including factors affecting pitch, loudness and quality.
(JMB only: **absorption of sound**, problems of sound transmission, insulation and noise suppression)

Multiple Choice Questions

Question 1 (O X F)
A person in a boat fires a pistol and hears the echo reflected from a cliff 3 s later. How far is he from the cliff? (Take the speed of sound in air to be 330 m/s.)

A *55 m*
B *110 m*
C *220 m*
D *495 m*
E *990 m*

Answer: D
Sound travels from boat to cliff and back again (important point about echoes).

$$\text{Speed} = \frac{\text{distance}}{\text{time}}$$

$$330 \text{ (m/s)} = \frac{2 \times d}{3 \text{ (s)}}$$

$$d = 495 \text{ m}$$

Question 2 (A E B multiple completion)
When a string vibrates so as to produce a stationary wave, all parts of the string between two adjacent nodes are vibrating

1 *with the same amplitude*
2 *with the same frequency*
3 *in phase*

Answer: 2 and 3 only
Nodes are positions of no amplitude, and between them are *antinodes* which have maximum amplitude, so it should be obvious that **1** is wrong.

Question 3 (A E B)

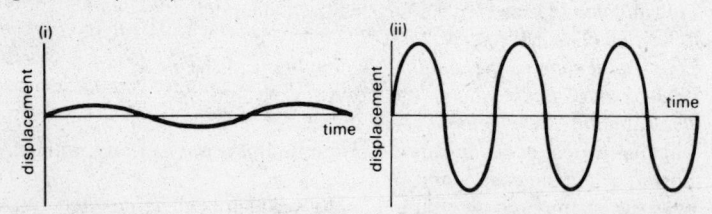

The above displacement/time graphs for two vibrating sources are drawn to the same scales. In comparison with graph (i), graph (ii) would represent a sound of

Waves, Sound and Light

A *higher pitch and lower intensity*
B *higher pitch and higher intensity*
C *lower pitch and lower intensity*
D *smaller wavelength and lower intensity*
E *lower pitch and higher intensity*

Answer: B
Pitch depends on *frequency*; (ii) has twice as many cycles in the same time as (i), so pitch must be higher. Intensity (loudness) depends on the amplitude of the wave; (ii)'s is greater than (i)'s so the intensity is higher.

Longer Questions

Question 1 (LON)
(a) What is the essential difference between a longitudinal wave and a transverse wave?
Why is the sound wave in air produced by a vibrating tuning-fork longitudinal? *(4 marks)*

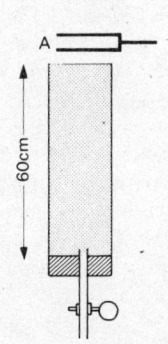

(b) A student holds a vibrating tuning-fork A which has the number 256 engraved on it just above a glass tube of length 60 cm containing water. The tube is allowed to slowly empty of water and the student hears a loud sound when there is 25·0 cm of water left in the tube. On repeating the experiment with tuning-fork B, which has the number 512 engraved on it, he hears a loud sound on two occasions as the tube empties of water.

(i) What is the meaning of the number 256 on tuning-fork A? *(2 marks)*
(ii) Explain why the student hears a loud sound when using fork A and state the name of this effect. *(4 marks)*
(iii) Use the figures given for tuning-fork A to calculate a value for the speed of sound in air. Suggest a reason why this value is only approximately correct. *(5 marks)*
(iv) Explain why, when using tuning-fork B, there were two occasions as the tube was emptying of water when a loud sound was heard, whereas with tuning-form A there was only one. *(5 marks)*

Answer
(a) In a **longitudinal wave** the vibration of the particles is in the same direction as the wave velocity.

Comment
See 'Vibrations and waves', p. 117.

In a **transverse wave** the vibration of the particles is at right angles to the wave velocity.

As the prongs of the vibrating tuning-fork move they alternately compress the air molecules together and give a pulse of rarefaction. These pulses are transmitted to neighbouring air molecules so that the wave moves with the vibrations of the air molecules in the same direction as the wave velocity.
(b) (i) The number 256 means that the frequency of the fork is 256 Hz.

(ii) When the water has emptied to such an amount that the natural frequency of the air column is the same as that of fork A, the air column will also be set into vibration with a large amplitude and a loud note will be heard. This effect is called **resonance**.

(iii) Length of air column at resonance = 60 − 25 = 35 cm

You must mention *compressions* and *rarefactions* of air molecules.

Don't forget to show that the vibrations are in the same direction as the wave velocity.

Probably one mark for the word 'frequency' and one for unit (Hz). In effect, this part of the question is just asking you what you mean by *resonance*.

Read the question carefully and realize that they give you the length of water left in the tube.

The diagram shows the fundamental mode of vibration for the pipe.

Here, $35(\text{cm}) = \dfrac{\lambda}{4}$

Since for a stationary wave

$\therefore \lambda = 140$ cm
$= 1{\cdot}4$ m

Remember, the first position of resonance is for $\dfrac{\lambda}{4}$.

Better to convert to metres here.

Since $v = f\lambda$
$v = 256(\text{Hz}) \times 1\cdot 4(\text{m})$

$= 358\cdot 4$ m/s

This value is only approximate since the end correction (due to the radius of the resonance tube and the distance between the tuning-fork and the end of the glass tube) has been ignored.

(iv) Using this value for v the position of first resonance can be found for the 512 Hz fork.

$v = f\lambda$
$358\cdot 4(\text{m/s}) = 512(\text{Hz}) \times \lambda$
$\lambda = 0\cdot 7$ m
∴ for the first position of resonance

$l_1 = \dfrac{\lambda}{4} = 0\cdot 175$ m

The second position of resonance is shown in the diagram; here,

$l_2 = \tfrac{3}{4}\lambda$
$l_2 = 0.525$ m

Since $l_2 < 60$ cm, both positions of resonance will be heard.

Wave equation: see p. 117.
Quote formula, then substitute numbers.

N.B. units.

The end correction is usually the reason for inaccuracies in resonance experiments.

This part of the question suggests that you are going to need both the first and second positions of resonance. So first calculate the new value for λ; second, find $\dfrac{\lambda}{4}$; and, third, find $\tfrac{3}{4}\lambda$.

Show that both values are less than 60 cm, so that both positions can be found.

Question 2 (AEB)

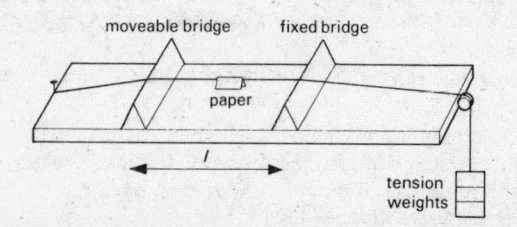

(a) The diagram shows a length of wire on a sonometer. A vibrating tuning-fork of frequency 256 Hz was placed on the wooden base of the sonometer, and the length l was adjusted until the small piece of paper jumped off the wire.

  (i) Explain why this happened.
  (ii) What is the name of this phenomenon? *(5 marks)*

(b) When the wire of the same sonometer is plucked it vibrates, emitting a note. State the effect on the fundamental frequency of this note, if

  (i) the length of the wire were halved with no change in the tension;
  (ii) the tension were made four times as large, with the original length unchanged;
  (iii) the wire in the diagram were replaced by one of mass per unit length four times as large, the length and tension being the same as in the first experiment. *(6 marks)*

(c) A student standing between two vertical cliffs, and 480 m from the nearest cliff, shouted. She heard the first echo after 3 s and the second echo 2 s later. Use this information to calculate:

  (i) the velocity of sound in air;
  (ii) the distance between the cliffs. *(8 marks)*

Answer
(a) (i) the length of the wire was changed until it reached a length with a natural frequency identical to that of the tuning-fork. It then vibrated with an amplitude great enough for the paper to fall off.

(ii) This phenomenon is called resonance.

Comment
Compare answer to question 1(b)(ii), p. 126.

Waves, Sound and Light 129

(b) For a sonometer, $f = \dfrac{1}{2l}\sqrt{\dfrac{T}{m}}$

A formula worth learning, from which you can then work out everything else.

(i) If l is halved with no change in T or m, then f is doubled (i.e. pitch rises an octave).

The remark in brackets isn't necessary, but if you know it, say it.

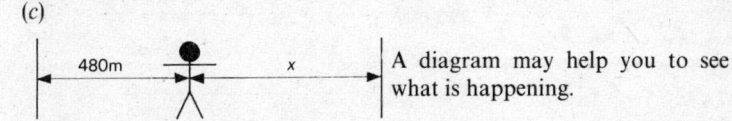

(ii) l is constant, m is constant and T is four times as large, so $f \propto \sqrt{T}$; f is therefore doubled and again the note rises an octave.

(iii) l is constant, T is constant and $f \propto \sqrt{\dfrac{1}{m}}$, so if m is four times as large then f is halved, i.e. is an octave lower.

(c)

A diagram may help you to see what is happening.

(i) First echo took 3 s.
Distance travelled by sound (to cliff and back) = $2 \times 480 = 960$ m

Remember: for all echo problems, sound must go there and back.

$$\text{Speed} = \dfrac{\text{distance}}{\text{time}} = \dfrac{960 \text{(m)}}{3 \text{(s)}}$$

Quote formula and substitute.

$= 320$ m/s

(ii) For second echo:
distance = $2x$ time = 5 s

N.B. second time = 3(s) + 2(s)
= 5 s

$$\text{Speed} = \dfrac{\text{distance}}{\text{time}}$$

$$320 \text{(m/s)} = \dfrac{2x}{5 \text{(s)}}$$

$x = 800$ m
∴ the distance between the cliffs
= 480 + 800 = 1280 m

Remember to look at what the question asks, and don't think x is the answer.

Electromagnetic Waves

Comparison of **light** with **sound**.
The continuity of the **electromagnetic spectrum**; **radio**, **infrared**, **visible**, **ultra violet**, **X-rays**, and **γ-rays**. Their common velocity in a vacuum and ordering in terms of frequency.
Colour and **frequency**.
Common properties of the electromagnetic spectrum and characteristic differences.

These subjects are more often covered by multiple choice questions and short-answer questions than by longer answer questions.

Multiple Choice Questions

Question 1 (AEB multiple completion)

| gamma rays | X-rays | ultra violet | infrared | radio waves |

visible spectrum

The diagram illustrates the electromagnetic spectrum. Moving from left to right across it corresponds to increasing

1 *frequency*
2 *velocity*
3 *wavelength*

Answer: 3 only
The velocity of *electromagnetic waves* is constant. If you learn that *infrared* has a longer wavelength than *ultra violet*, this kind of question will be easy.

Question 2 (AEB multiple completion)
Infrared rays have the properties that they

1 are electromagnetic waves of lower frequencies than visible light
2 are emitted by hot bodies
3 can be detected using a Geiger–Müller counter

Answer: 1 and **2** correct
See answer to Question 1 and remember that if wavelength increases, the frequency will decrease, as the velocity of electromagnetic waves is constant. You are expected to know some properties of each kind of radiation.

Question 3 (LON)
A translucent white plastic bottle has green printing on it. An electric lamp with red glass is suspended inside the bottle and switched on in a darkened room. The green printing on the bottle will appear to be

A black
B blue
C magenta
D red
E yellow

Answer: A
The green filter (since light is inside the bottle) will not allow red light through, so the lettering will look black.

Question 4 (AEB)

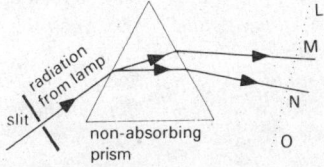

In an experiment on the spectrum of a high-power electric lamp, the blackened bulb of a thermometer was moved along the line LMNO across the refracted beam. M and N mark the limits of the visible parts of the spectrum. The thermometer gave the highest reading

A between L and M
B at M
C between M and N
D at N
E between N and O

Answer: A
The blackened bulb of the thermometer should suggest that you are looking at *infrared absorption*. Infrared is beyond the red end of the spectrum, i.e. LM.

Longer Questions

Question 1 (OXF)
Radio transmission is possible with a certain spectrum of waves that travel through space at 3×10^8 m/s.

(a) Draw a diagram of the completed electromagnetic spectrum, labelling the various types of radiation. *(3 marks)*
(b) State two differences between radio waves and the other types of radiation in the electromagnetic spectrum. *(2 marks)*
(c) What is the importance of the ionosphere in radio-wave propagation? *(2 marks)*

(d) What is the frequency of the radio transmission on wavelength 1500 m?

Answer

(a) See diagram for Question 1, p. 130.

(b) (i) They have a longer wavelength.

(ii) They are formed by high-frequency oscillatory electric currents.

(c) The radio waves are reflected off the ionosphere, and so can travel further round the earth.

(d) $v = f \times \lambda$ (wave equation)
$3 \times 10^8 \text{(m/s)} = f \times 1500\text{(m)}$
$f = 2 \times 10^5$ Hz

Comment

You are expected to know the difference between kinds of radiation in the *electromagnetic spectrum*. Only 2 marks, so don't go into lots of detail.

This is really the only possible way the ionosphere could help.

See p. 117.
State formula and substitute numbers. You are only given v and λ, so *wave equation* should immediately spring to your mind.

Question 2 (A E B part question)

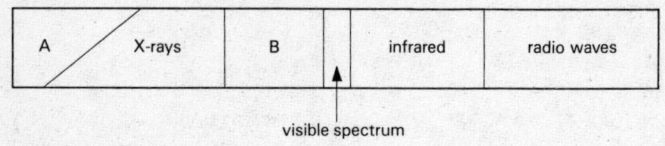

| A | X-rays | B | infrared | radio waves |

↑ visible spectrum

The diagram shows the regions of the electromagnetic spectrum.

(i) Name the region A.

(ii) Name the region B.

(iii) In which region, A or B, does the radiation possess the higher set of frequencies?

(iv) The radiations in all the regions are transverse electromagnetic wave motions and have one property in common. Name this property.

Answer

(i) γ-rays.
(ii) Ultraviolet.
(iii) A.
(iv) They all move with the same velocity in a vacuum.

Comment

'Name', so do no more than this. Look for what is missing if you do not immediately know the answer. See comment on Question 1 above.

An important point about the electromagnetic spectrum.

Geometric Optics

This is a very large section in all the syllabuses, so it will be studied in four parts:

(a) Straight line propagation
(b) Reflection
(c) Refraction
(d) Interference and diffraction

(a) Straight line propagation
Rectilinear propagation of light.
Pinhole camera.
Shadows with point and extended sources.

Multiple Choice Questions

Question 1 (A E B)

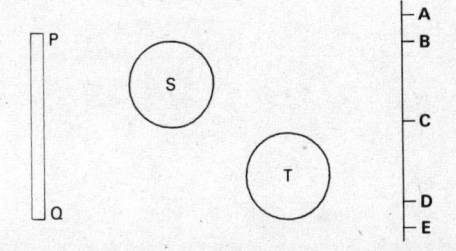

PQ represents an extended source of light and S and T are opaque objects Which one of the points **A, B, C, D** *or* **E** *on the screen is totally dark?*

Answer: D
Put your ruler on each point in turn, and see if you can reach a part of PQ without going through S or T. You can for every point *but* **D**.

Question 2 (OXF)

A pinhole camera is used to form an image of an object of height h at a distance d from the pinhole as shown in the diagram. The angle at the pinhole between rays from the top and the bottom of the object is θ. The camera is of length l. In order to calculate the height of the image formed at the back of the camera, which of the following pairs of quantities is sufficient?

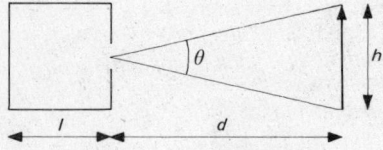

A l *and* θ
B θ *and* d
C d *and* l
D l *and* h
E h *and* d

Answer: A

If you considered this problem in terms of similar triangles you would need all three distances shown. As you are only given two quantities θ must be one of the necessary pair. As the rays spread out again from the pinhole the length *l* must also be known in order to find the height of the image.

Longer Questions

Question 1

Describe an experiment to show that light travels in a straight line.

Answer

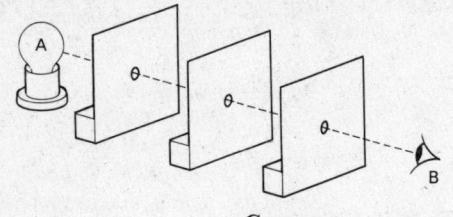

Three cardboard screens have small holes in them level with each other at the same distance from their base. They are set so that they are in a straight line by threading

Comment

Remember, 'describe' should immediately make you draw a diagram.

Say what your diagram is showing.

some cotton through the holes and pulling it taut. A lamp is then placed as shown and can be seen by an eye placed at B. If one of the screens is slightly moved, the light can no longer be seen. If it is moved back so that the light is now seen, it can be checked that the screens are again in a straight line.

It is worth pointing out that when the screens are *out* of line the light cannot be seen.

(b) Reflection

Laws of reflection: (i) the **incident ray**, the **reflected ray** and the **normal** all lie in the same plane; (ii) the **angle of incidence** is equal to the **angle of reflection**.

Image formation in a plane mirror including ideas of **image position**, **lateral inversion** and **virtual image**.

Spherical mirrors of small aperture: **converging (concave)** and **diverging (convex)**.

Principal axis, pole, principal focus, focal length, centre of curvature, radius of curvature.

Radius of curvature = 2 × focal length.

Determination of focal length and radius of curvature of a converging (concave) mirror.

Use of ray diagrams for determining the nature, size and position of images formed by converging and diverging mirrors. (Calculation is also allowed for solving problems.)

Linear magnification: $\dfrac{\text{size of image}}{\text{size of object}} = \dfrac{\text{distance of image to mirror}}{\text{distance of object to mirror}}$.

Multiple Choice Questions

Question 1 (LON)

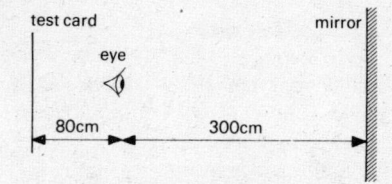

An optician's test card is fixed 80 cm behind the eyes of a patient, who looks into a plane mirror 300 cm in front of him, as shown in the diagram above. The distance from his eyes to the image of the card is:

A 300 cm	**Answer: D**
B 380 cm	The image is as far behind the mirror as the object is in front of it, i.e. 380 cm, so it is $380 + 300 = 680$ cm from the eye.
C 600 cm	
D 680 cm	
E 760 cm	

Question 2 (AEB)

An observer using a converging (concave) mirror locates an inverted image of the same size and at the same position as the object. Which one of the following conclusions is justified?

A Only rays parallel to the axis can form images.
B The object is at the centre of curvature of the mirror.
C Concave mirrors never produce erect images.
D Such a mirror can only produce virtual images.
E The object is nearer the pole of the mirror than the focal point.

Answer: B
A and C do not seem to follow as conclusions, so they can be ignored. You need to know where virtual images are produced (i.e. for E), since distractors such as this often occur.

Question 3 (AEB multiple completion)

Light which is incident on a plane mirror at an angle of 30° to the normal is reflected:

1 at an angle of 60° to the mirror
2 on the opposite side of the normal
3 in the same plane as the incident ray and the normal

Answer: 1, 2 and 3

Waves, Sound and Light 137

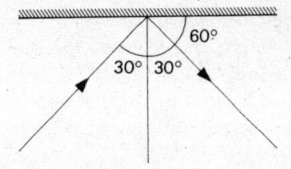

A diagram may help you to see that
1 and **2** are true.
3 is one of the *laws of reflection*.

Longer Questions

Question 1 (AEB part question)

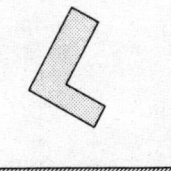

The diagram shows a letter L on a horizontal piece of paper on which a plane mirror is placed vertically.
(i) Copy the diagram on your paper and draw suitable rays to locate the image of the corner of the letter L nearest to the mirror.
(ii) On your diagram draw the image of the letter L. (5 marks)

Answer

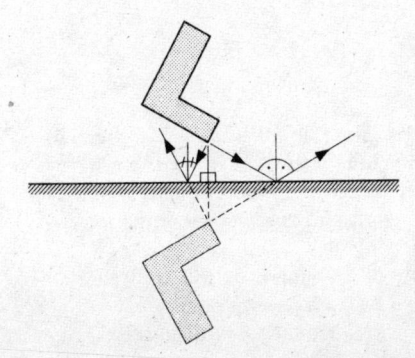

Comment
Make sure you put arrows on the rays to show which is incident and which reflected. Dot back the reflected rays to find the image portion. It may help to fold the paper along the mirror line in order to see what the image should look like for part (ii).

Question 2 (OXF)

(a) State the laws of reflection for light meeting a mirror, and use them to predict the reflected path of one ray meeting a concave spherical mirror.
(3, 3 marks)
(b) An observer close to a large concave mirror sees an enlarged upright image of himself. Draw a ray diagram to show how one point (not on the axis) of this image is formed *(4 marks)*
(c) Describe an experiment in which, by making the image coincide with the object, the focal length of a concave mirror may be found. What is measured and how is the result calculated? *(6 marks)*
(d) A bright object 50 mm high stands on the axis of a concave mirror of focal length 100 mm and at a distance of 300 mm from the concave mirror. How big will the image be? *(4 marks)*

Answer

(a) (i) The incident ray, the reflected ray and the normal all lie in the same plane.
(ii) The angle of incidence is equal to the angle of reflection.
A ray from the centre of a concave spherical mirror will be reflected along its own path, since the radius of a circle is at right angles to the tangent of a circle; i.e. both the angle of incidence and the angle of reflection are zero.
(b)

Comment
Learn these laws.

The easiest ray to consider is one from the centre of the sphere.
N.B. you can consider the sphere as a circle because of law (i) (p. 135).

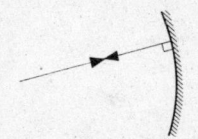

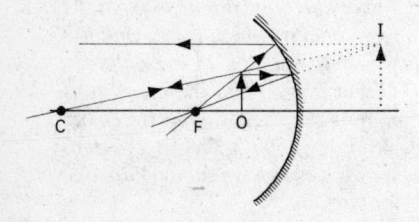

'Close to mirror' should remind you that the object must be between F and the mirror for an upright image. Two of the following rays only are essential:
(i) through C and O and reflected back on its own path,
(ii) through O parallel to the prin-

cipal axis and reflected back through F,
(iii) through F and O reflected parallel to the principal axis.
Since the image is upright, you should expect it to be *virtual* and to have to dot back the reflected rays.

'Describe an experiment' should immediately make you think of a diagram.

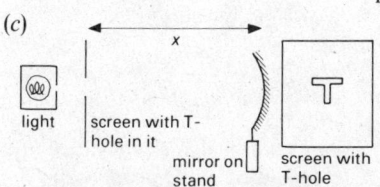

(c)

The apparatus is set up as shown in the diagram so that the centre of the mirror and the T-hole are at the same level. The mirror is moved until a clear image of the T (upside down) can be caught on the screen beside the T. The distance x between the mirror and the screen is then measured. This distance is the **radius of curvature** of the mirror and is twice the focal length:

$$\therefore f = \frac{x}{2}$$

Describe in words as well as with a diagram.

Remember to say the image will be upside down.

(d) The graphical solution:
The image is 25 mm high,

The formula solution:
using the convention that *real is positive*,
$u = 300$ mm $f = 100$ mm $v = ?$

$$\frac{1}{v} + \frac{1}{u} = \frac{1}{f}$$

$$\frac{1}{v} + \frac{1}{300} = \frac{1}{100}$$

$$\frac{1}{v} = \frac{3}{300} - \frac{1}{300} = \frac{2}{300}$$

$\therefore v = 150$ mm

Magnification $= \frac{v}{u} = \frac{150}{300} = 0.5$

∴ the image is half the object's size, i.e. 25 mm high.

In graphical solutions:
(1) draw rays as suggested in part (b),
(2) give scales – remember that the vertical and the horizontal scales need not be the same,
(3) don't forget to translate the answer in terms of your scale.
State sign convention.

Quote formula and substitute to find v, then use *magnification* $= \dfrac{\text{image size}}{\text{object size}} = \dfrac{v}{u}$ to find the image size.

(c) Refraction
Refraction at a plane surface.
Refractive index $_a\mu_m$ or $_a n_m = \dfrac{v_a}{v_m} = \dfrac{\lambda_a}{\lambda_m} = \dfrac{\sin i}{\sin r} = \dfrac{\text{real depth}}{\text{apparent depth}}$.
All definitions need to be known.
Laws of refraction: (i) the incident ray, the refracted ray and the normal all lie in the same plane; (ii) the ratio of the sine of the angle of incidence to the sine of the angle of refraction is a constant.
Total internal reflection and **critical angle**. Thin spherical lenses of small aperture: **converging (convex)** and **diverging (concave)**.
Principal axis, centre, principal foci, focal lengths (power in dioptres, J M B only).

Determination of the focal length of a converging lens.
Use of ray diagrams for determining the nature, size and position of images formed by converging and diverging lenses.
Graphical solutions or calculations allowed.
(Colour is studied under 'Electromagnetic waves', p. 130–32, and optical instruments under 'Optical instruments and applications', p. 148–54.)

Multiple Choice Questions

Question 1 (LON matching pairs)
In each of the diagrams below, parallel rays of light fall on a simple piece of optical equipment contained in a 'black box'.

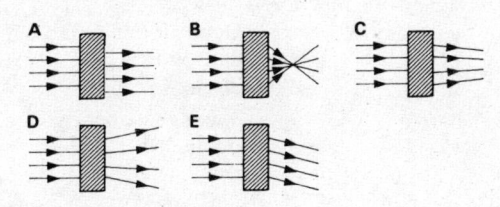

In which diagram does the box contain
(i) *a rectangular glass block?*

Answer: A
Rays emerge parallel to each other and to the *incident rays* but 'shifted' sideways.

(ii) *a diverging lens?*

Answer: D
The only diagram where the rays spread out (*diverge*).

(iii) *a weak converging lens?*

Answer: C Rays *converge*, i.e. come together, so the answer is either **B** or **C**: and **C** is obviously the weaker of the two.

Question 2 (AEB multiple completion)
For which of the following object distances, in cm, will a converging (convex) lens of focal length 30 cm produce a final image which is enlarged, virtual and the same way up as the object?

1 12
2 24
3 36

Answer: 1 and 2 only
The object must be between F and the lens to produce such an image. (There are a lot of questions on this idea.)

Question 3 (LON multiple completion)
When light travelling in a more dense medium is incident at an interface with a less dense medium it may be

1 refracted
2 partially reflected
3 totally internally reflected

Answer: 1, 2 or 3 correct
You should remember that **3** only occurs when going from a *more* dense medium to a *less* dense medium.

Longer Questions

Question 1 (LON)
(a) In an experiment to determine the refractive index of a glass block, several values for the angles of incidence, i, and refraction, r, were obtained and listed in the following table.

Angle of incidence	$i/°$	9	20	30	46	62
Angle of refraction	$r/°$	6	15	21	30	40
sin i						
sin r						

(i) Copy the table and complete by inserting values for sin i and sin r in the table. Use these results to plot a straight line graph. *(8 marks)*
(ii) Calculate the refractive index for the glass block. *(3 marks)*

Waves, Sound and Light 143

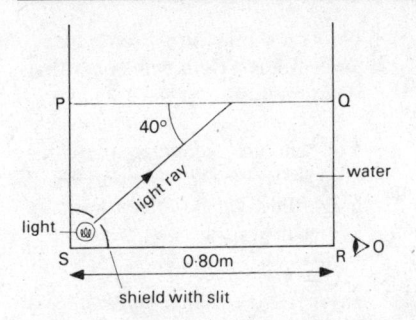

(b) The diagram shows a side view of a water-filled aquarium PQRS. An electric lamp, surrounded by a shield with a narrow slit, is immersed in one corner of the aquarium at S. The light ray from the slit shines on the water surface PQ at an angle of 40° as shown.

(i) If the refractive index of water is 1·33, calculate the critical angle for a ray travelling from water to air. *(3 marks)*

(ii) Draw a diagram of the light ray shown above meeting the water surface PQ, and show its path after meeting the surface. Calculate the angle this new path makes with PQ and label the angle. *(3 marks)*

(iii) The shield surrounding the lamp is turned slightly, so that when an observer O looks perpendicularly at the side QR the lamp is directly visible. Calculate how far the image of the lamp appears to be from QR. *(3 marks)*

Answer

(a)
Angle of incidence	$i/°$	9	20	30	46	62
Angle of refraction	$r/°$	6	15	21	30	40
$\sin i$		0·156	0·342	0·500	0·719	0·883
$\sin r$		0·105	0·259	0·358	0·500	0·643

Graph of $\sin i$ against $\sin r$ for glass block

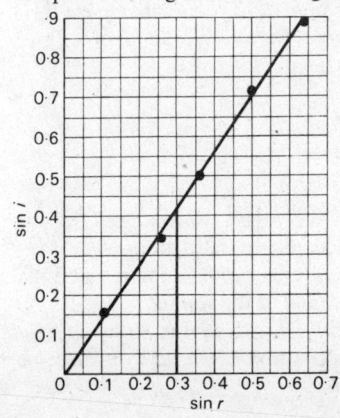

Comment

Use calculator or sine tables to complete table.

Don't forget to give the graph a title and to label its axes. Not all the points lie on the straight line. Draw in the line 'of best fit'. It must go through the origin, and should have the points off it (i.e. points 2 and 4) on either side of it.

Examiners reported that people had difficulty in drawing the line as required.

144 Passnotes: **Physics**

The **refractive index** of glass is defined as the ratio of $\dfrac{\sin i}{\sin r}$, which is the gradient of the graph.

$$\text{R.I. of glass} = \frac{0\cdot 42}{0\cdot 3}$$

$$= 1\cdot 4$$

(b)(i) The **critical angle** is the angle of incidence such that the angle of refraction is 90°. The light must be travelling from a more dense medium to a less dense medium.

$$\frac{\sin c°}{\sin 90°} = {}_w n_a$$

$${}_w n_a = \frac{1}{{}_a n_w} \text{ and } \sin 90° = 1$$

$$\therefore \frac{1}{{}_a n_w} = \sin c$$

$$\frac{1}{1\cdot 33} = \sin c$$

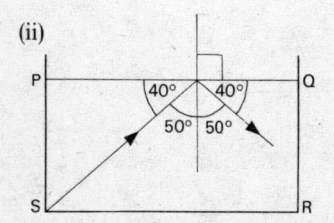

$$c = 48\cdot 75°$$

(ii)

Since 50° > 48·75° the angle of incidence is greater than the *critical angle*, so **total internal reflection** will occur. This new path, therefore, also makes an angle of 40° with PQ.

Quote formula for *refractive index*. Since R.I. is a ratio, remember that it has no units.

You should recognize that this answer is of the right order of magnitude. Do not give too many figures in your answer.

Say what the *critical angle* is, and so derive the formula.

${}_w n_a$ – refractive index from water to air. You are given ${}_a n_w$ – the refractive index from air to water.

From part (i) you might expect this part of the question to involve *total internal reflection*.

Don't forget that angles of incidence *and* refraction are always measured between the ray and the normal to the surface.
Only 3 marks for drawing *and* calculation of angle, so it must be easy.

(iii) $_a n_w = \dfrac{\text{real depth}}{\text{apparent depth}}$ Quote formula and substitute.

$$1\cdot 33 = \dfrac{0\cdot 80 \text{(m)}}{x}$$

$$x = \dfrac{0\cdot 80}{1\cdot 33} = 0\cdot 60 \text{ m}$$

∴ the light appears to be 0·60 m from QR.

Question 2 (L O N)

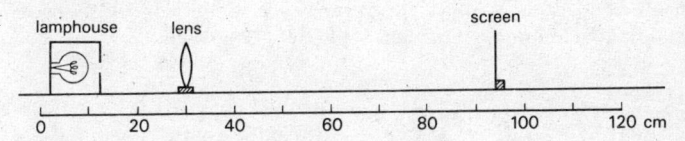

A lamphouse containing a filament lamp was fixed on a bench in front of a convex lens as in the diagram. A white screen was adjusted until a sharp image of the filament was obtained. The positions of the lamp, lens and screen on the bench were noted in the table of results below. The lens and screen were moved and a second set of readings obtained.

Position of filament (cm)	Position of lens (cm)	Position of screen (cm)	Object distance (cm)	Image distance (cm)	Magnification
8·0	30·0	96·0			
8·0	71·0	92·0			

(i) Copy and complete the table of results. Compare the sizes of the two images obtained. (6 marks)

(ii) Using the first set of readings above, determine a value for the focal length of the lens. (5 marks)

(iii) Explain why it was impossible to adjust the screen to obtain an image when the lens was placed at the 20 cm position on the bench. How can an image of the filament be seen with the lens in this position? Briefly describe the appearance of the image seen. (6 marks)

Answer

(i)
Position

Position of filament (cm)	Position of lens (cm)	Position of screen (cm)	Object distance (cm)	Image distance (cm)	Magnification
8·0	30·0	96·0	22·0	66·0	3
8·0	71·0	92·0	63·0	21·0	$\frac{1}{3}$

Comments

Magnification = $\dfrac{v}{u}$

v = image distance
u = object distance

∴ the first image is nine times as large as the second.

(ii) $\dfrac{1}{f} = \dfrac{1}{u} + \dfrac{1}{v}$

$\dfrac{1}{f} = \dfrac{1}{22 \cdot 0} + \dfrac{1}{66 \cdot 0}$

$= \dfrac{3+1}{66 \cdot 0} = \dfrac{4}{66 \cdot 0}$

$f = \dfrac{66 \cdot 0}{4} = 16 \cdot 5 \text{ cm}$

You should know this formula for the London board.

Remember units

(iii) If the lens is at the 20 cm mark the object distance would be 12·0 cm, which is less than the focal length, so a real image cannot be found. A virtual image is formed as shown in the diagram.

Since an image cannot be caught on the screen you should expect a virtual image, and you should know that it is only formed for a convex lens if the object is nearer the lens than its focus.

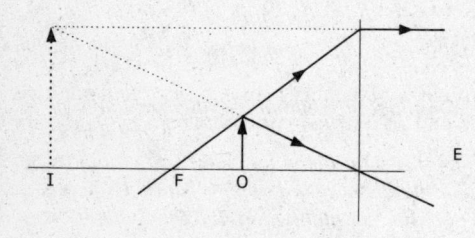

If an eye is placed at E the image of the filament will be seen. It will be enlarged, and the same way up as the original object.

Two rays needed: one through F and refracted parallel to the principal axis and one through the centre of the lens. As they diverge they must be dotted back to find the image. A diagram will help you to explain the last part, too.

(d) Interference and diffraction

Though this topic does appear in several syllabuses, it is examined at length under 'vibrations and waves' (pp. 117–23); there are very few questions on it, so only one will be discussed here.

Dispersion of light by a finely ruled grating; single-slit **diffraction of light**. **Interference** by a double-slit arrangement; comparison of patterns obtained by light of different wavelengths.

Estimation of the order of magnitude of the wavelength of visible light by a simple double-slit experiment.

Question 1

Explain why the fringe pattern seen in a Young's slits experiment is as shown below if monochromatic red light is used. What would be the difference in the pattern if monochromatic blue light were used? What would this tell you about the difference between red and blue light? If the wavelength of the red light used in the experiment above was 6.5×10^{-7} m and the screen was 4 m from the slits, the fringe separation was found to be 1.3 cm. What is the slit separation?

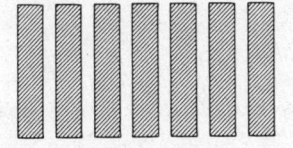

Shaded area is red and unshaded area is black.

Answer

The light waves from the two slits interfere. When two waves are superposed in the same phase, e.g. crest on crest or trough on trough, there is increased disturbance and a bright red light is seen, because **constructive interference** is occurring.

When the waves are superposed exactly out of phase, e.g. crest on trough, there is **destructive interference**, i.e. no disturbance, and darkness is seen. These fringes are equally spaced.

Comment

Make sure you explain clearly the difference between *constructive* and *destructive* interference.

With blue light the fringes will be closer together.

This shows that the wavelength of blue light is less than that of red light.

Fringes will either be closer or more spread out! Since $w = \dfrac{\lambda D}{a}$, i.e. $w \propto \lambda$, and you should know that λ red $> \lambda$ blue, you expect the fringes to be closer together (w-fringe separation, a-slit separation).

$w = \dfrac{\lambda D}{a}$ where w is fringe separation, λ is wavelength, D is distance from screen to slits and a is slit separation.

$$0{\cdot}013 \,(m) = \dfrac{6{\cdot}5 \times 10^{-7} \,(m) \times 4 \,(m)}{a}$$

$$a = \dfrac{6{\cdot}5 \times 10^{-7} \times 4}{0{\cdot}013}$$
$$= 0{\cdot}0002 \,m \,(= 0{\cdot}02 \,mm)$$

Quote formula and substitute values. You should have some idea of the order of magnitude of the answer. Remember to work in metres throughout.

Optical Instruments and Applications

These vary from board to board, so do be sure to look at your syllabus to see what is required.
Driving mirrors.
Single lens camera. Prism binoculars.
Simple slide projector.
The eye as an optical instrument.
Magnifying glass.
Astronomical telescope, Newtonian reflection telescope and radio telescope of the parabolic reflection type (these last three are J M B only).

Multiple Choice Questions

Question 1 (L O N)
When a ray of light, travelling in air, is incident obliquely at an optically denser material it is refracted towards the normal. Which of the following actions does NOT make use of this effect?

A Film projection using a convex lens
B Formation of a spectrum using a 60° prism
C Formation of an image on a film by a camera lens
D Magnification produced by a magnifying glass
E Production of a shadow when a cloud passes in front of the sun

Answer: E
All the others are examples of practical uses of refraction. In **E** the light is cut off by the cloud, thus forming a shadow, rather than passing obliquely into a different medium.

Question 2 (A E B multiple completion)
The image of a slide produced by a projector is

1 real
2 enlarged
3 the same way up as the slide

Answer: 1 and 2 only
Anyone who has ever shown holiday slides knows that they must be put in the projector upside down, but that the picture can be caught on the screen and is enlarged.

Question 3 (A E B multiple completion)

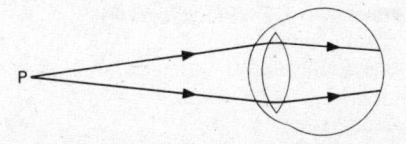

The diagram illustrates a defective eye which is fully accommodated. P is the near point for a normal eye in the same position as this eye.

1 The eye is 'long-sighted'.
2 Its near point is further away than P.
3 The defect can be remedied by converging (convex) spectacle lenses.

Answer: 1, 2 and 3 true
It is important to know about defects of the eye as well as the way the eye works.

Longer Questions

Question 1 (LON)
(a) A camera is used to photograph a small statue 80 cm high which is 500 cm away from the camera lens. The distance between the lens and the film is 5 cm. Without making any calculation, what can be deduced about the focal length of the lens? Account for your answer. *(4 marks)*
Determine the height of the image produced on the film. *(3 marks)*
If the camera is now used to photograph a distant scene, what adjustment would need to be made? *(2 marks)*
Draw a ray diagram to show how a lens similar to that in the camera may be used as a magnifying glass. Mark on the diagram the position of the observer's eye. *(6 marks)*
(b) A person finds that in order to read a newspaper easily he must hold it at arm's length, although he can see distant objects quite normally. Name the defect from which he is suffering. Suggest a possible cause of the defect. Explain how this defect may be overcome by the use of suitable spectacle lenses. *(5 marks)*

Answer
(a) The *focal length* of the lens must be less than 5 cm. This is because the image in a *convex* lens is only formed past the *focal point*. For very distant objects the image is at the focal point.

$$\text{Magnification} = \frac{\text{image size}}{\text{object size}}$$

$$= \frac{\text{distance between image and lens}}{\text{distance between object and lens}}$$

$$\frac{\text{image size}}{80 \text{(cm)}} = \frac{5 \text{(cm)}}{500 \text{(cm)}}$$

∴ image size = 0·8 cm

For a distant scene, the lens must be moved so that the distance between it and the film is its focal length.

Comment
You need a knowledge of where images are formed in *convex* lenses; see 'Refraction', pp. 140–48.

Two formulae to be known.

Now substitute numbers in question.

A small diagram might help to make your answer clear.

Waves, Sound and Light 151

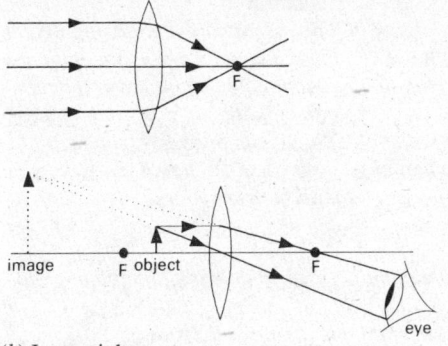

Show position of object, image and eye clearly. Mark in the path of the light rays.

'Name': there is no need for more.

(b) Long sight.
The eyeball may be too short. This can be overcome using a converging lens as shown below.

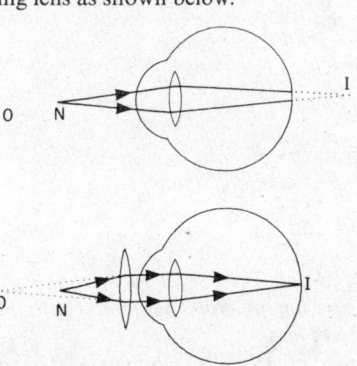

Question 2

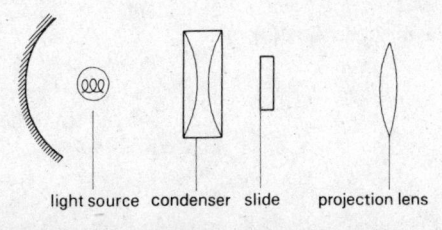

Describe the purpose of the condenser and the projection lens in the slide projector shown in the diagram above. *(4 marks)*

152 *Passnotes:* **Physics**

Answer

The condenser collects the light, which would otherwise spread out from the source, and directs it all through the slide.

The projection lens can be moved to and fro so that the image can be focused on the screen.

Comment

This is one of the most important points about a slide projector, so you should know how the condenser works.

You have probably adjusted the position of this lens if you have ever tried to show slides.

Question 3 (AEB)

(a) A converging (convex) lens can be used to produce an upright image of an object.

(i) Draw a ray diagram to show how this image is formed.

(ii) State whether this image is real or virtual.

(iii) Name one practical use of a converging (convex) lens used in this manner. *(5 marks)*

(b)

object of height 5mm

object lens of focal length 20mm

eye lens of focal length 30mm

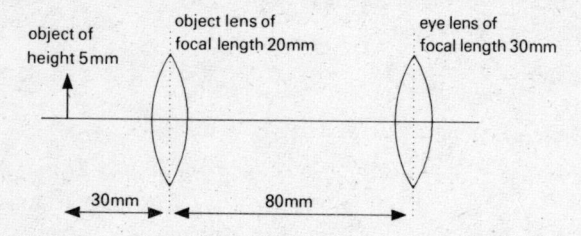

30mm   80mm

The diagram shows an arrangement of an object and two lenses.

(i) Find, by calculation or by construction on graph paper, the position and size of the image formed by the object lens.

(ii) This image acts as an object with respect to the eye lens. Find the position and size of the image produced by the eye lens. *(8 marks)*

Answer

(a) (i) See answer to Question 1(a), p. 150.

(ii) Virtual.

Comment

The rays had to be dotted back as they diverged from the lens, so the image is *virtual*.

(iii) It can be used as a magnifying glass.

You will probably have learnt the diagram for this use.

(b) (i) Assume *real is positive* convention.

By calculation: $u = +30$ mm
$v = ?$
$f = +20$ mm

$$\frac{1}{v} + \frac{1}{u} = \frac{1}{f}$$

Quote formula.

$$\frac{1}{v} + \frac{1}{30} = \frac{1}{20}$$

Substitute.

$$\frac{1}{v} = \frac{1}{20} - \frac{1}{30} = \frac{1}{60}$$

$v = 60$ mm, i.e. image is 60 mm behind the object lens.

Remember units.

Magnification $= \frac{v}{u} = \frac{60}{30} = 2$

∴ image size is 10 mm.

By graph:

Remember to show scales, and that vertical and horizontal scales need not be the same.

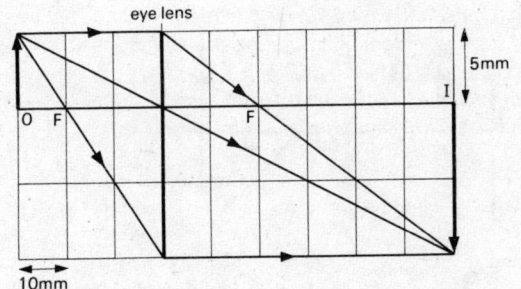

image size = 10mm   image distance = 60mm

3 rays drawn – put arrows on rays and draw in image.

(ii) This image is 20 mm from the eye lens.

By calculation: $u = +20$ mm
$f = +30$ mm
$v = ?$

$$\frac{1}{v} + \frac{1}{u} = \frac{1}{f}$$

$$\frac{1}{v} + \frac{1}{20} = \frac{1}{30}$$

$$\frac{1}{v} = \frac{1}{30} - \frac{1}{20} = -\frac{1}{60}$$

$$v = -60 \text{ mm}$$

The image is virtual and 60 mm in front of the eye lens (and 20 mm behind the object lens).

$$\text{Magnification} = \frac{v}{u} = \frac{60}{20} = 3$$

∴ image size is 30 mm.

By graph:

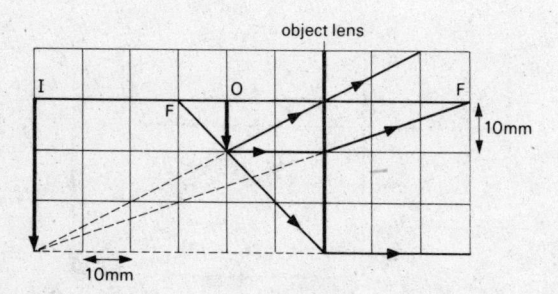

The image is virtual, 30 mm high and 60 mm from the eye lens (20 mm from the object lens).

This arrangement is like a compound microscope, so you can expect a virtual image.

General Questions

Multiple Choice

These questions are mostly in the form of matching pairs.

Question 1 (L O N)
The following are five optical components:
A concave mirror
B convex mirror
C converging lens
D diverging lens
E plane mirror

(i) Which of the above is represented by the line XY in the following diagram? (O is the object and I is the image.)

Answer: D
Since the light passes through XY it cannot be a mirror. The top ray turns away from the second ray which should suggest divergence of the rays.

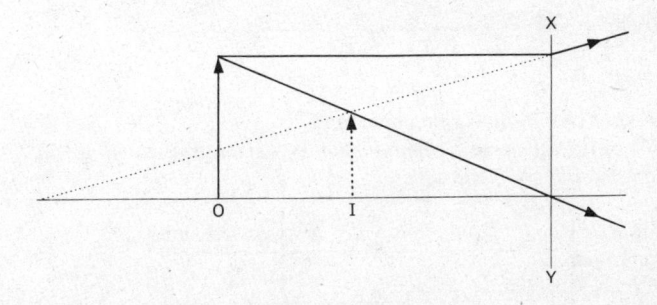

(ii) Which of the above is represented by XY in the diagram overleaf? (O is the object and I is the image.)

Answer: B
Here the rays are obviously reflected by XY, so the answer must be A, B or E. E can be rejected as the upper ray would be reflected back on its own path. Since the image is formed behind the mirror, but is smaller than the object, XY must represent a convex mirror.

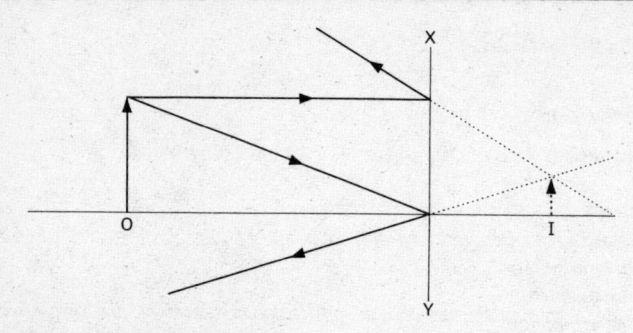

(iii) For which can an inverted image be formed which is in the same position as its object?   **Answer: A**

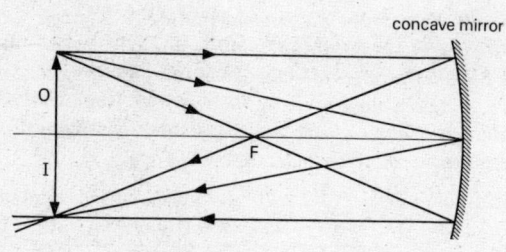

Question 2 (AEB multiple completion)
Which of the following phenomena can be demonstrated with a 90°, 45°, 45° glass prism and white light?

1 *Refraction*
2 *Dispersion*
3 *Internal reflection*

Answer: **1, 2 and 3**

Longer Questions

Question 1 (LON)
(a) In an attempt to determine the refractive index of the glass of a prism, a student directs a narrow beam of white light perpendicularly towards the side AB as shown opposite.

  (i) By describing what happens to the light as it passes into, through and out of the prism, explain why the student will find it impossible to determine a value for the refractive index of the glass using this arrangement.

Waves, Sound and Light 157

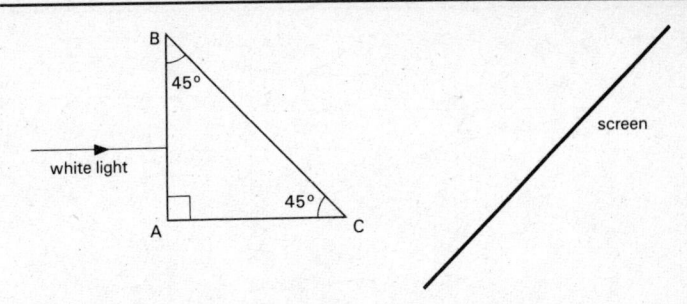

(ii) Draw a diagram showing the path taken by the light into, through and out of the prism.

(iii) Give reasons why the light behaves in the way you have described in (a) (i). *(6 marks)*

(b) In a further experiment the student replaces the prism shown in the diagram by one with $\hat{B} = 30°$ and $\hat{C} = 60°$.

(i) Draw a separate diagram to show how this prism produces a spectrum on the screen. State the name of the colour which is deviated most.

(ii) Calculate the angle of emergence from the side BC of the colour for which the glass has a refractive index of 1·53.

(c) The speed of light in air is $3·0 \times 10^8$ m/s and the mean refractive index of glass is 1·5. Calculate the speed of light in glass.
What effect if any does this change of speed have on
(i) the frequency and
(ii) the wavelength of the light as it passes through the glass? *(4 marks)*

Answer

(a) (i) Since the light meets AB at right-angles there is no refraction and it passes through undeviated until it reaches BC. Here, since it strikes BC at an angle of incidence larger than the critical angle, it is totally internally reflected and therefore meets AC at right-angles and passes out of the prism undeviated. The light, therefore, is turned through 90° and has not been refracted by the glass/air or air/glass boundaries, so the refractive index cannot be determined.

Comment

Make sure you include 'into, through and out of the prism'.

Also explain why you cannot determine refractive index using this set-up.

158 *Passnotes:* **Physics**

(ii)

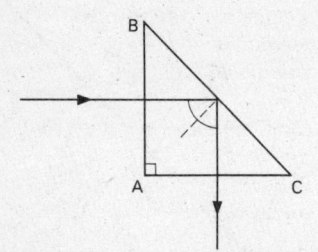

Show that the angles of incidence and reflection are equal.

(iii) When light is refracted from a more dense medium to a less dense medium, e.g. glass to air, the light is bent away from the normal. The angle of refraction is larger, therefore, than the angle of incidence. If the angle of incidence is large enough the angle of refraction becomes 90°, and the light is refracted along the boundary between the two mediums. When the angle of incidence is even larger, the angle of refraction is so large that the light remains in the first medium and is totally internally reflected.

This is asking you to explain total internal reflection. You may find that diagrams help you explain. If so, helpful ones would be:

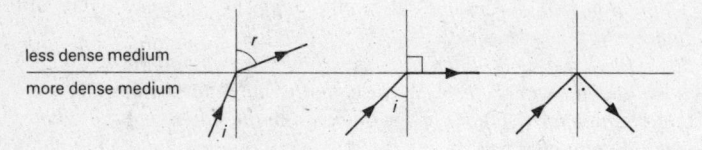

(b)
(i)

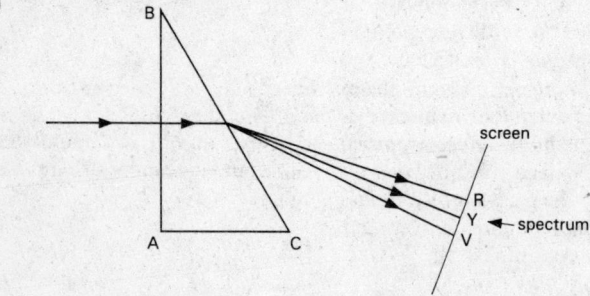

Waves, Sound and Light 159

The violet is deviated most.
(ii)

[Diagram: ray entering prism at B with 60° and 30° marked, angle r inside, angle e at exit toward C]

$$_gn_a = \frac{\sin i}{\sin r}$$

$$_an_g = \frac{1}{_gn_a}$$

$$\therefore {_an_g} = \frac{\sin r}{\sin i}$$

$$1\cdot53 = \frac{\sin r}{\sin 30}$$

$$\sin r = 0\cdot5 \times 1\cdot53$$

$$r = 49\cdot9°$$

∴ the light emerges at 40·1° to BC.

(c) The refractive index of glass
$$= \frac{\text{speed of light in air}}{\text{speed of light in glass}}$$

$$1\cdot5 = \frac{3\cdot0 \times 10^8 \text{ (m/s)}}{v}$$

$$v = 2\cdot0 \times 10^8 \text{ m/s}$$

The change in speed has no effect on the frequency, but reduces the wavelength of the light as it passes through the glass.

Remember, there will still be no refraction at AB, but at BC the colours will split up.

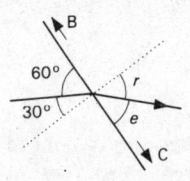

Don't miss out this statement.

Don't forget the angle of incidence from the geometry of the prism.

'Refractive index of glass' means $_an_g$. Here, your light ray is going from glass to air, so you must adjust for this.

See diagram above for relationship between r and e.

See p. 144.
Quote formula and then substitute numbers given.

Frequency only depends on the source of the light, so it is unaffected. Since $v = f \times \lambda$, if v is reduced then λ must also be reduced.

Section 6: Electricity and Magnetism

Power Sources

This section is not included in all syllabuses and the amount of detail required varies greatly, so do look at your own syllabus to see what you need to know.

The voltaic effect between dissimilar **electrodes** in an **electrolyte** (i.e. principles behind **simple cells**).

Zinc–carbon dry cell, **lead–acid** cell: basic construction and characteristics in use, i.e. **e.m.f.** (the amount of energy converted from chemical or dynamic energy to electrical energy per unit charge), **internal resistance** and effects of **polarization.**

Capacity in ampere-hours of a **secondary cell.**

Low voltage mains power unit and its structure (see also under 'Domestic electricity supply', pp. 182–7).

The simple generator is covered in 'Electromagnetic induction', pp. 176–82.

Multiple Choice Questions

Question 1 (AEB)
The e.m.f. of a cell is quoted as 1·5 V. This means the cell can supply 1·5

A *amperes of current*
B *coulombs of charge*
C *joules of energy*
D *joules of energy per ampere of current it delivers*
E *joules of energy per coulomb of charge it delivers*

Answer: E
This is a definition of e.m.f. see above.

Question 2 (multiple completion)
Which of the following is (are) secondary cell(s)?

1 Daniell cell
2 Simple cell
3 Lead–acid accumulator

Answer: 3 only
A secondary cell can be recharged, so **1** and **2** must be wrong.

Question 3 (LON)
It was intended to electroplate with copper a metal disc which was about 4 cm in diameter. A circuit was assembled exactly as shown in the diagram and the metal disc was carefully cleaned and suspended from a wire in the electrolyte. The switch was closed and the current indicated by the ammeter A was adjusted to a suitable value by means of a rheostat R. After 20 minutes the current was switched off and the disc was removed, rinsed and dried.

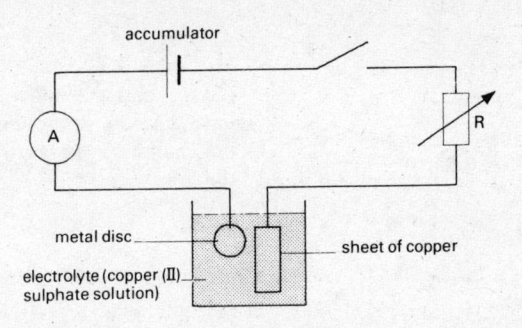

(a) It was found that no copper had been deposited on the disc. This was because

A hydrogen bubbles formed on the sheet of copper
B the accumulator connections were incorrect
C the concentration of the electrolyte was incorrect
D the resistance of the electrolyte was too high
E the process requires alternating current

Answer: B
Remember: copper will only be deposited on the *cathode*, so the disc must be attached to the *negative* pole of the accumulator.

(b) The reason for cleaning the disc before putting it into the electrolyte was to

A enable the disc to be weighed accurately
B ensure that the deposited copper would adhere well
C prevent hydrogen forming on the disc
D prevent impurities contaminating the electrolyte
E reduce the resistance to the flow of current through the bath

Answer: B
Though several of the other distractors sound convincing, this is the reason you always clean things which are to be *electroplated*.

(c) The plate in the bath which connects with the negative terminal of the accumulator would be referred to as the

A anode
B cathode
C diode
D node
E pole

Answer: B
The other words are all used in physics, and are put in in case you have a vague knowledge of them but cannot remember which is the right answer.

Longer Questions

This topic is rarely set as a complete long question, so only one example will be given.

Question 1 (LON part question)
Many electronic calculators can be powered either by using dry cells or by connecting through an adaptor to the domestic electricity supply.

(a) Why is an adaptor necessary? Without giving details of its electrical circuit, explain briefly how it works. (4 marks)
(b) Draw a labelled diagram of a dry (Leclanché) cell. (6 marks)
(c) State one advantage and one disadvantage of using the mains supply rather than a battery to power the calculator. (2 marks)

Electricity and Magnetism

Answer
(a) The calculator works on a lower voltage than that of the a.c. mains and on *direct current*. A *step-down transformer* will reduce the voltage and a *diode* and a *smoothing circuit* will transform the a.c. to d.c.

Comment
Two parts here:
(i) too high voltage, and
(ii) a.c. rather than d.c.
State them both as problems and deal with each in your adaptor.

(b)

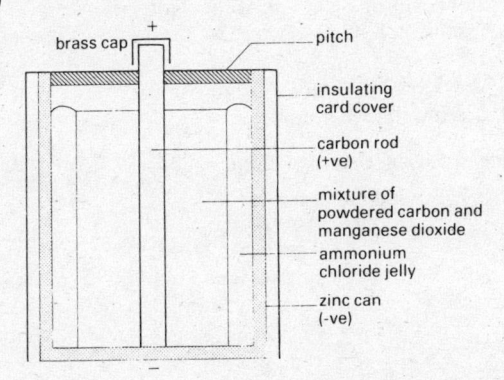

- brass cap
- pitch
- insulating card cover
- carbon rod (+ve)
- mixture of powdered carbon and manganese dioxide
- ammonium chloride jelly
- zinc can (-ve)

No need to explain how it works. Picture a dry cell, and you should be able to draw most of this from general use; though of course you will have to know the chemicals involved.

(c) An advantage is that your mains supply never runs down or needs replacing. A disadvantage is that the calculator is much less portable.

Sheer common sense and being used to using calculators!

Currents in Circuits
The idea of electric current using **d.c. sources.**
The **conservation of charge** (and so current) at junctions.
Current = charge/unit time (unit: **ampere**).
Electromotive force, which measures the energy/unit charge produced from a d.c. source as it converts some other sort of energy to electrical energy.

Potential difference between two points is the work done in taking the unit charge between the two points (Unit: **volt**, i.e. **joule/coulomb**).

Resistance: the ratio of the potential difference across a component to the current flowing through it (unit: **ohm**).

Resistors in **series** and **parallel** ($R = R_1 + R_2$ in series; $\frac{1}{R_1} + \frac{1}{R_2} = \frac{1}{R}$ in parallel); **internal resistance** of power source.

Measurement of resistance by ammeter and voltmeter methods.

Ohm's law: the resistance of a conductor is constant at constant temperature.

Variation of resistance with temperature.

Use of the thermistor as a simple thermometer.

Heating effect of an electric current (work done $= VIt = I^2Rt = \frac{V^2t}{R}$).

Resistivity and its measurement.

Comparison of p.d. by potentiometer (OXF only).

Multiple Choice Questions

This is a very popular section for multiple choice setters, so several examples are given here.

Question 1 (AEB)
What is the potential difference in V across the 3 Ω resistor?

A $\frac{1}{9}$
B $\frac{1}{2}$
C 1
D $\frac{6}{5}$
E 2

Answer: C
Total *resistance* in circuit
$= 1 + 3 + 2 = 6\,\Omega$
$V = IR$ for whole circuit,
i.e. $2 = I \times 6$
$I = \frac{1}{3}$ A
For 3 Ω resistor:
$V = \frac{1}{3} \times 3 = 1$ V
(or V across 3 Ω resistor
$= \frac{3}{6} \times 2$ V $= 1$ V)

Question 2 (LON)
How much electric charge runs through a lamp in 5 minutes when a steady current of 2 A is passed through it?

A 2·5 C
B 10 C
C 150 C
D 600 C
E 1200 C

Answer: D

$$\text{Current} = \frac{\text{charge}}{\text{time}}$$

$$\therefore \text{Charge} = \text{current} \times \text{time}$$
$$= 2(A) \times (5 \times 60)(s)$$
$$= 600 \text{ C}$$

N.B. time must be measured in seconds.

Question 3 (LON Matching pairs)

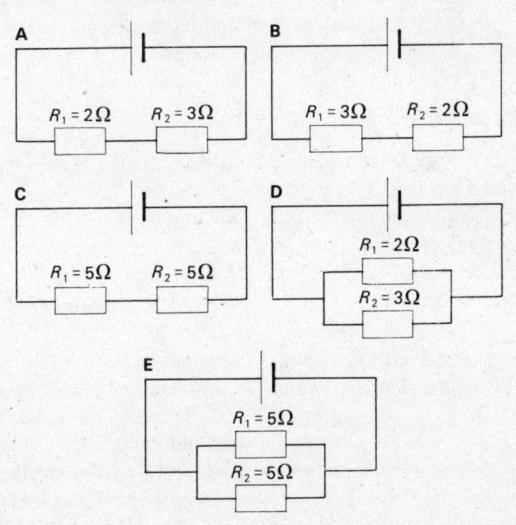

The diagrams show five circuits, in each of which the resistors R_1 and R_2 are connected to a cell with an e.m.f. of 2 V and of negligible internal resistance. The values of R_1 and R_2 are given in each circuit.

(i) In which circuit will the current in R_1 be different from that in R_2?

Answer: D
The current is the same for resistors in series, so it must be **D** or **E**; and **D** is the one with different values for R_1 and R_2.

(ii) In which circuit is the effective resistance smallest?

Answer: D
In *series*, $R = R_1 + R_2$; in *parallel*,
$$\frac{1}{R} = \frac{1}{R_1} + \frac{1}{R_2}$$
∴ resistance will be smaller for parallel circuits.

D: $\dfrac{1}{R} = \dfrac{1}{2} + \dfrac{1}{3}$ ∴ $R = \dfrac{6}{5}\,\Omega$

E: $\dfrac{1}{R} = \dfrac{1}{5} + \dfrac{1}{5}$ ∴ $R = \dfrac{5}{2}\,\Omega$

(iii) A 250 mA fuse is connected next to the cell in each circuit; in which circuit will the fuse NOT blow?

Answer: C
The fuse blows if the current is larger than its value. Current is smallest for largest resistance.
$R_A = 5\,\Omega\ \ R_B = 5\,\Omega\ \ R_C = 10\,\Omega$
$R_D = \tfrac{6}{5}\,\Omega\ \ R_E = \tfrac{5}{2}\,\Omega$
For **C:** $V = IR$
$\qquad\qquad 2 = I \times 10$
$\qquad\qquad I = 0{\cdot}2\,\text{A} = 200\,\text{mA}$

(iv) In which circuit will the current through the 2 V cell be 0·8 A?

Answer: E
$V = IR$
$2 = 0{\cdot}8 \times R$
$R = 2{\cdot}5\,\Omega$ (see answer above)

(v) In which circuit will the voltage across R_1 be smaller than the voltage across R_2?

Answer: A
For **D** and **E**, voltage across R_1 and R_2 is the same, as they are in parallel.
In **C**, R_1 and R_2 are the same, so voltage must be the same.
$V = IR$, ∴ $V \propto R$, so we want $R_1 < R_2$, i.e **A**.

Question 4 (AEB multiple completion)
The resistance of a metal wire is increased by increasing its

1 temperature
2 length
3 cross-sectional area

Answer: 1 and 2
$R = \dfrac{\rho l}{A}$; so as cross-sectional area is increased, resistance decreases.

Question 5 (AEB)
A resistance coil used as a thermometer has a resistance of 10.0 Ω when immersed in melting ice and 12.0 Ω in boiling water. Its resistance is 11.4 Ω when placed in another substance. The temperature in °C of this substance is

A 14
B 20
C 30
D 70
E 140

Answer: D
You can do this either as a heat question or from your knowledge of the variation of resistance with temperature.

$$\frac{R_\theta - R_0}{R_{100} - R_0} = \frac{\theta}{100}$$

$$\frac{11 \cdot 4 - 10 \cdot 0}{12 \cdot 0 - 10 \cdot 0} = \frac{\theta}{100} \quad \therefore \theta = 70$$

Longer Questions

Question 1
What is the resistance of an electrical component? How would you measure the resistance of a piece of resistance wire?

Answer
(a) The *resistance* of an electrical component is the ratio of the *potential difference* across it to the *current* flowing through it.

Comment
A definition that needs to be learnt by heart.

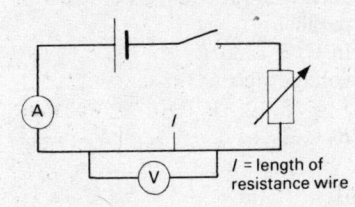

The circuit is set up as shown above.
The rheostat is moved to six different settings, and in each case the readings on the ammeter and the

Always draw a circuit diagram. You want more than one set of readings of V and I, so include a rheostat.

voltmeter are noted. The key is held down for as short a time as possible to reduce heating effects.

A graph is drawn of potential difference (reading on V) against current (reading on A). A straight line through the origin should be obtained, and the gradient of this graph $\left(\dfrac{\Delta V}{\Delta I}\right)$ will give the resistance of the wire,

$$R = \frac{\Delta V}{\Delta I}$$

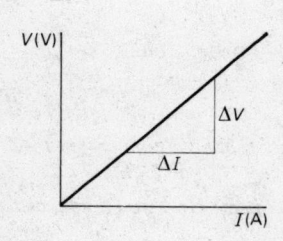

This precaution should always be mentioned in resistance measurement experiments.

Always say what shape of graph you expect to obtain.

A diagram is often the easiest way to explain how to work out the gradient of a graph.

Question 2 (LON)

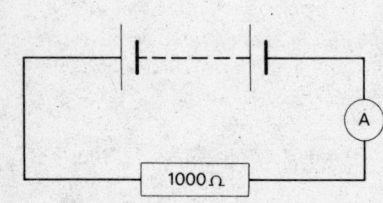

A large battery is connected as shown to a resistor of resistance 1000 Ω. The potential difference across the resistor is 50 V.

(i) What is the reading on the ammeter? (2 marks)
(ii) How many coulombs of charge are supplied by the battery in 1 minute? (2 marks)
(iii) Calculate the energy dissipated by the resistor in this time. (2 marks)
(iv) What is the power dissipated by the resistor? (2 marks)

Electricity and Magnetism 169

Answer
(i) Across resistor: $V = IR$
$50(V) = I \times 1000(\Omega)$
$I = 0.05$ A
This is the reading on the ammeter.

(ii) Current = $\dfrac{\text{charge}}{\text{time}}$

$0.05(A) = \dfrac{\text{charge}}{60\,(s)}$

charge = 3 C

(iii) Energy in resistor = I^2Rt
$= 0.05(A) \times 0.05(A) \times 1000(\Omega)$
$\times 60\,(s)$
$= 150$ J

(iv) Power dissipated by resistor
$= VI$
$= 50\,(V) \times 0.05\,(A)$
$= 2.5$ W

or power = $\dfrac{\text{energy}}{\text{time}} = \dfrac{150(J)}{60(s)}$
$= 2.5$ W

or power = I^2R
$= 0.05\,(A) \times 0.05\,(A) \times 1000\,(\Omega)$
$= 2.5$ W

Comment
This question requires you to remember a lot of formulae – quote them and substitute numbers. Be careful with units.

N.B. time must be in seconds. Remember, units of charge are coulombs (C).

Any of these methods is quite satisfactory.

Question 3 (OXF)
A cell of internal resistance 0.8 Ω is connected in series with ammeters A_1 and A_2 and a lamp as shown below. A voltmeter V_1 is connected across the cell and a voltmeter V_2 is connected across the lamp. The reading of A_1 is 0.3 A and that of V_2 is 1.2 V.
(Assume that the ammeters have negligible resistances and that the voltmeters draw negligible currents.)

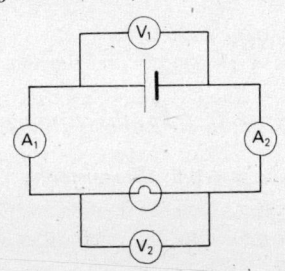

(a) Find the resistance of the lamp. (3 marks)
(b) Find the reading of V_1. (1 mark)
(c) What is the reading of A_2? (1 mark)
(d) Find the electromotive force (e.m.f.) of the cell. (3 marks)

Answer

(a) P.d. across lamp = V_2 = 1·2 V
Current through lamp = A_1 = 0·3 A

$$R = \frac{V}{I}$$

∴ resistance of light $= \dfrac{1\cdot 2 \,(V)}{0\cdot 3 \,(A)}$
$= 4\,\Omega$

(b) Since A_1 and A_2 have negligible resistance, V_1 and V_2 will read the same because they are reading the same p.d., i.e. reading on V_1 = 1·2 V.

(c) A_2 reads the same as A_1 as both have the same current through them.
∴ reading on A_2 = 0·3 A

(d) For the whole circuit
e.m.f. = $IR + Ir$
= $V_{\text{lamp}} + Ir$
= 1·2 (V) + 0·3 (A) × 0·8 (Ω)
= 1·2 (V) + 0·24 (V)
= 1·44 V

Comment

It may help to put the numerical information given in the question into the diagram.

The diagram looks confusing, but if you ignore A_1 and A_2 the two voltmeters can be seen to be connected in the same place.

The current throughout the circuit is the same unless there are parallel junctions.

E.m.f. should make you think about the whole circuit. N.B. since they give you *internal resistance (r)*, you know you must use it in whole-circuit problems.

Elementary Magnetism

Elementary properties of magnets and behaviour of soft iron and steel.
Magnetic fields: representation by lines using both iron filings and compass methods; uniform and non-uniform fields; direction of fields.
Magnetic fields due to single bar magnet, a single straight conductor carrying an electric current, a plane coil and a solenoid.
Effect of the presence of magnetic materials within a magnetic field.

Electricity and Magnetism

Qualitative treatment of force on a current in a uniform field and force between current-carrying wires.

Force on a moving charged particle in a magnetic field. (See also 'Moving charges', pp. 190–94).

Multiple Choice Questions

Question 1 (LON)
A length of insulated wire is held between the poles of a strong horseshoe magnet and a current is passed through the wire in the direction shown in the diagram.

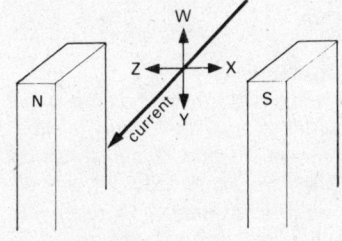

The wire will experience

A *a force in the direction of W (upwards)*
B *a force in the direction of X (towards S pole)*
C *a force in the direction of Y (downwards)*
D *a force in the direction of Z (towards N pole)*
E *no force because of the effects of the insulation*

Answer: A
Use *Fleming's Left-hand Rule.*

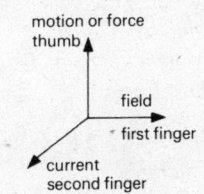

Question 2 (AEB)
Which of the following operations would tend to reduce the permanent magnetic properties of a bar magnet?

1 *Cooling it to about* $-30°C$
2 *Hammering it with a mallet*
3 *Placing it in a solenoid carrying an alternating current and then slowly removing it*

Answer: 2 and 3 only
Remember: *molecular theory of magnetism*: order for magnetic, disorder for non-magnetic. Cooling tends to produce order, while the others both lead to more disorder.

Question 3 (OXF)

Two conducting wires X and Y lie side by side a short distance apart and parallel to one another. Wire X carries a current of 3 A, whilst wire Y carries a current of 5 A (as shown in the diagram) and each exerts a force upon the other.

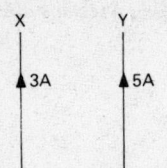

If the current in Y were to be reversed, then

A only the force on X would be reversed

B only the force on Y would be reversed

C the forces on both wires would be reversed

D the forces on both wires would be unchanged in both direction and magnitude

E the forces on both wires would be unchanged in direction but decreased in magnitude

Answer: C
The important thing to remember with two *current-carrying conductors* is: current same direction, wires are attracted; current different directions, wires repel each other.

Longer Questions

This section is rarely used for a complete long question, but it is popular for parts of questions or short answer questions.

Question 1 (LON part question)

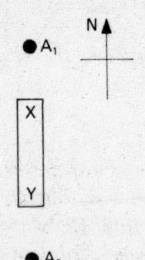

The diagram shows a bar magnet XY on a laboratory bench. When a small plotting compass is moved around the magnet, it is found that there are two positions A_1 and A_2 where the plotting compass will set in any direction.

(i) What is the polarity of the end X of the magnet?

(ii) What is the name given to the positions A_1 and A_2?

Electricity and Magnetism 173

(iii) Why will the plotting compass set in any direction at A_1 and A_2?
(iv) If the magnet is rotated so that X and Y are interchanged, where must the plotting compass be placed in order that it will again set in any direction?
(7 marks)

Answer
(i) End X must be a south pole.
(ii) A_1 and A_2 are called *neutral points*.
(iii) At A_1 and A_2 the force on the plotting compass due to the bar magnet's field is exactly balanced by the force on it due to the earth's magnetic field.

Comment
Only 7 marks in all, so just give answers; don't bother to explain. In fact, if you can't remember which end X should be, think how a neutral point is formed by equal and opposite fields and draw rough diagrams to help you.

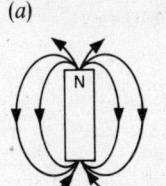

(a)   (b)

You will see that only in (b) could you have a *neutral point* at A_1 and A_2.

(iv)
When the magnet is rotated neutral points will be at A_3 and A_4.

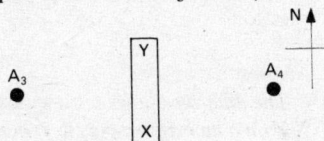

Now use the rough diagrams to help you find neutral points in (a), and you will see that they have to be at the sides of the magnet (about the same distance from the magnet as A_1 and A_2).

Question 2

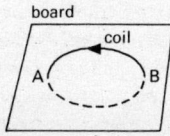

The diagram shows a vertical thin circular coil with a steady current flowing from B to A as shown. Draw the magnetic field due to the current in the coil as you would see it on the board. You may neglect any effect of the Earth's magnetic field.

Answer

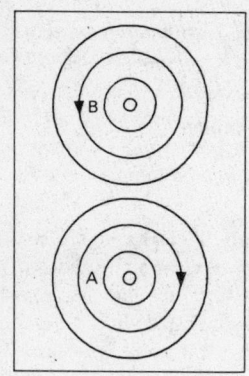

Comment
Remember the *right-hand grip rule* to help you with direction.

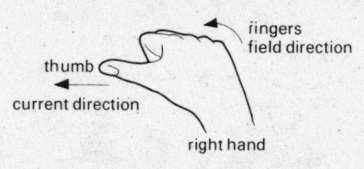

Electromagnetic Devices

Electromagnets.
Moving-coil loudspeaker, the electric bell, simple relay.
Moving-coil galvanometer and its conversion for the measurement of current and voltage.
d.c. motor.

Multiple Choice Questions

Question 1 (LON multiple completion)
Which of the following devices make(s) use of the magnetic field generated by an electric current?

1 Electric iron
2 Moving-coil galvanometer (or ammeter)
3 Electric bell

Answer: 2 and 3 only
1 uses the heat energy associated with an electric current, not the magnetic field.

Question 2 (AEB multiple completion)
The polarities of the ends of an electromagnet depend upon the

1 *direction of the current in the coil*
2 *magnitude of the current in the coil*
3 *number of turns of wire in the coil*

Answer: 1 only
The other distractors affect the strength of the electromagnet, but not the polarity.

Electricity and Magnetism

Question 3 (AEB multiple completion)
Which of the following is true of a moving-coil voltmeter?

1 *It is placed in series with other apparatus in a circuit.*
2 *It should have a high internal resistance.*
3 *It may have its range increased by use of a resistance in series.*

Answer: 2 and **3** only
Always remember: a *voltmeter* is placed in *parallel* with a component in a circuit.

Longer Questions

Question 1
Draw a simple d.c. electric motor and mark in clearly the direction of the current and the direction of rotation of the armature. How could you increase the speed of the motor? *(12 marks)*

Answer

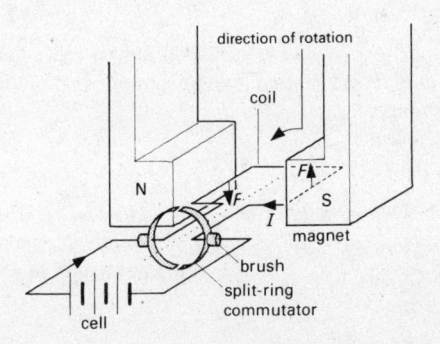

The speed of the motor depends on the force acting on the sides of the coil and the distance between them. It can be increased by increasing the current in the coil, the strength of the magnet, the number of coils or the area of the coil.

Comment
You may well have experienced this practically by altering the current in a motor and seeing its speed change. Probably only one of these is needed.

Question 2 (AEB)
A student is required to measure currents up to 1·00 A. He is given a reel of wire of resistance 0·5 Ω/m and a moving-coil galvanometer of resistance 10 Ω which has a full-scale deflection for a current of 0·01 A. Explain how the student could adapt the galvanometer in order to measure the required range of currents. *(10 marks)*

Answer
The wire must be used as a *shunt*, i.e. a resistance placed in parallel with the galvanometer.

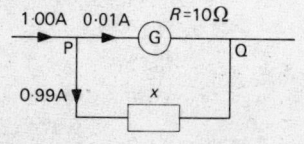

Comment
Say first of all whether you want a *shunt* or a *multiplier*.

A diagram will help you to solve the problem. Put in the currents in each branch of parallel arrangement.

The p.d. between P and Q is V.
$$V = IR = 0.01 \text{ (A)} \times 10 \text{ (Ω)}$$
$$= 0.99 \text{ (A)} \times x \text{ (Ω)}$$

$$\therefore x = \frac{0.01 \times 10}{0.99}$$
$$= 0.101 \text{ Ω}$$

The wire has a resistance of 0·5 Ω/m so he will need $\dfrac{0.101 \text{ (Ω)}}{0.5 \text{ (Ω/m)}}$

$$= 0.202 \text{ m}$$

of wire to make the shunt.

Since they tell you the resistance/metre of the wire, you should work out what length of wire is needed.

Electromagnetic Induction

Factors affecting **induced electromotive force and current** and their experimental demonstration. This usually includes interactions between two solenoids, a solenoid and a permanent magnet, and the effect of rotating a magnet in or near a solenoid.

Lenz's Law: the direction of the induced e.m.f. is such as to oppose the change producing it.

Electricity and Magnetism

Simple single-phase **a.c. generators** (alternators), both rotating-coil and rotating-magnet types (use of commutator to modify to d.c. generator). Moving-coil microphone and magnetic record pick-ups (AEB, CAM).
Alternating current: its nature and its frequency.
Transformers: structure, operation, turns ratio, primary and secondary power, sources of **energy loss** and ways to minimize these.
Transmission of electrical energy by the National Grid; the advantage of using high voltage and d.c.

Multiple Choice Questions

Question 1 (AEB)
The N pole of a long bar magnet was pushed slowly into a short solenoid connected to a galvanometer. The magnet was held stationary for a few seconds with the N pole in the middle of the solenoid and then withdrawn rapidly. The maximum deflection of the galvanometer was observed when the magnet was

A   about to enter the solenoid
B   moving into the solenoid
C   at rest inside the solenoid
D   being withdrawn
E   completely withdrawn

Answer: D
You should remember doing this practically, and that the speed of cutting magnetic flux affects the induced e.m.f.

Question 2 (AEB)
A transformer which is 80 per cent efficient gives an output of 10 V and 4 A. What is the input power, in W?

A   25
B   32
C   40
D   50
E   200

Answer: D
Power = $V \times I$
output power = 10(V) × 4(A)
= 40 W
This is 80 per cent of input power since

$$\text{efficiency} = \frac{\text{output power}}{\text{input power}}$$

$$\therefore 0.8 = \frac{40 \text{ W}}{\text{input power}}$$

input power = 50 W

Question 3 (LON)

A coil P is connected to a centre-zero galvanometer. A second coil Q is placed above the first as shown and connected to a battery, rheostat R and switch S.

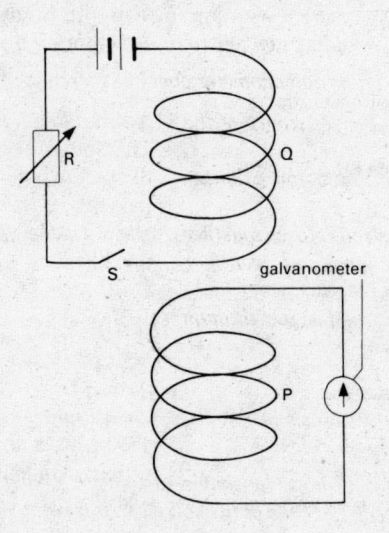

Which of the graphs below best represents the deflection of the galvanometer when the switch is closed for a few seconds and then opened?

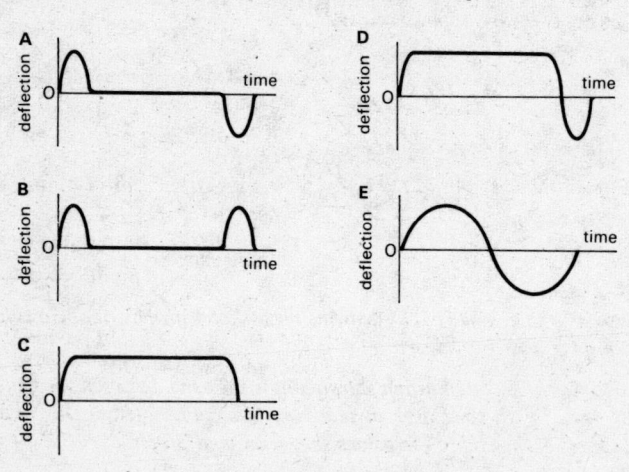

Electricity and Magnetism 179

Answer: A
Remember: e.m.f. is only induced when the magnetic flux is *changing*, and *Lenz's Law* suggests that the deflections will be in opposite directions.

The deflection of the galvanometer could be increased most by

A   increasing the resistance of the rheostat R
B   keeping S closed for a longer period
C   moving the coils closer together
D   putting a long soft iron bar through both coils
E   putting a long steel bar through both coils

Answer: D
The soft iron bar would increase the magnetic flux linkage between the coils. (The steel bar would not allow *changes* in flux to occur so quickly.)

Longer Questions

Question 1 (LON)
(a) The diagram shows a simple generator. Explain why an e.m.f. is produced between the ends of the coil when it is rotated. *(4 marks)*

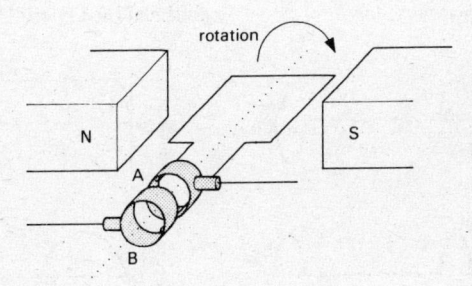

Answer (i), (ii) and (iii) by drawing three sketch graphs, one below the other on a sheet of graph paper.

(i) Draw a sketch graph showing how the e.m.f. between the ends of the coil varies with time over at least one revolution of the coil. Relate the positions of the coil to the values shown on your graph. *(4 marks)*

(ii) Draw a sketch graph showing what you would expect if the speed of rotation of the coil were doubled. *(2 marks)*

(iii) Draw a sketch graph showing what you would expect if, in addition to rotating at twice the speed, the coil contained twice as many turns.

(2 marks)

The output from the generator is found to be unsuitable for charging a car battery. Why is this? What modification to the generator would be necessary to enable this to be done? *(4 marks)*

(b) A power-station generator produces an e.m.f. of 33 000 V at a frequency of 50 Hz. The domestic supply is approximately 250 V, 50 Hz. Explain how the output of the power station can be modified for use in the home.

(4 marks)

Answer

(*a*) As the coil rotates, its sides cut the magnetic flux and an e.m.f. is induced. The direction of the e.m.f. is from A to B (using **Fleming's Right-hand Rule**).

Comment

Fleming's Right-hand Rule

first finger — field
second finger — current
thumb — motion

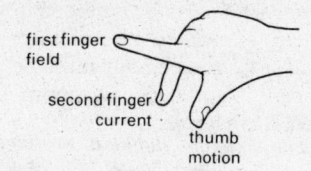

(i)

Mark in positions where coil is vertical and horizontal.

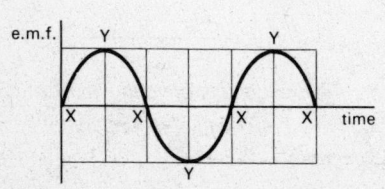

At X, coil is vertical; at Y, coil is horizontal

(ii)

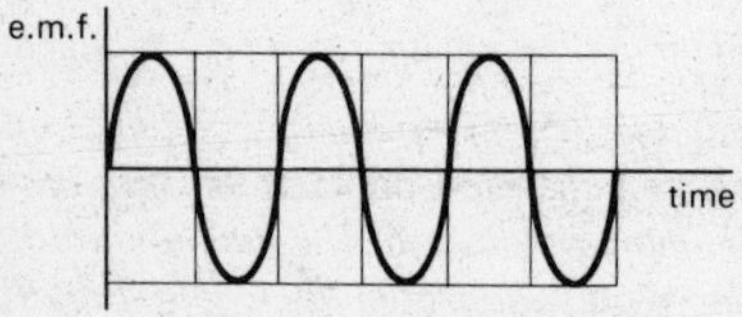

Doubling the speed of rotation will mean that it is in the vertical and horizontal positions twice as often.

Electricity and Magnetism 181

(iii)

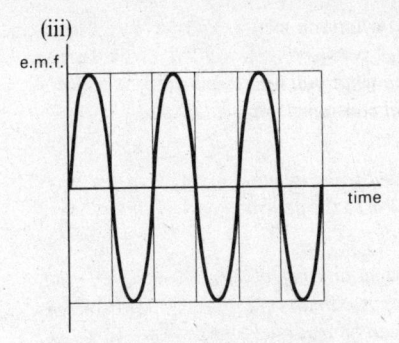

Doubling the number of coils will double the peak e.m.f. Don't forget to keep the frequency the same as the second graph.

The output from this generator is removed using slip rings, so it is an a.c. voltage. To charge a car battery, a d.c. voltage is needed. A split-ring commutator is needed to produce a rectified a.c. voltage, and a smoothing circuit must be included to produce an approximate d.c. voltage.

The examiners complain that *split-ring* and *slip-ring commutators* are often confused and poorly explained.

Remember: split-ring commutator for motors and d.c. generators.

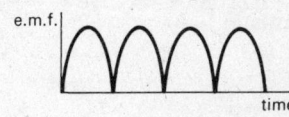

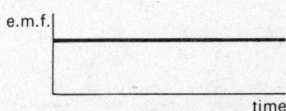

The diagram above shows rectified a.c. voltage. You need to add a smoothing circuit to bring it nearer to a d.c. voltage as shown below.
A diagram will show that you know what a transformer is.

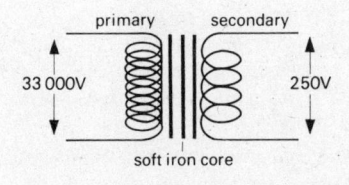

(b) A step-down transformer is needed.

Assuming an ideal transformer:

$$\frac{\text{no. of turns in secondary}}{\text{no. of turns in primary}} = \frac{\text{e.m.f. in secondary}}{\text{e.m.f. in primary}}$$

i.e. required turns ratio $= \dfrac{250}{33\,000}$

Since they give you the numbers, work out the *turns ratio*.

Question 2 (AEB part question)
A transformer has 400 turns on the primary coil and 10 turns on the secondary coil. If the primary e.m.f. is 240 V and the current in the secondary circuit 4 A, and assuming that there is no loss of energy, calculate
  (i) the secondary e.m.f.
  (ii) the primary current.
State one way in which energy is lost in a transformer.

Answer

(i) If there is no loss in energy:
$$\frac{\text{e.m.f. in secondary}}{\text{e.m.f. in primary}} = \frac{\text{no. of turns in secondary}}{\text{no. of turns in primary}}$$

$$\frac{\text{e.m.f in secondary}}{240 \text{ (V)}} = \frac{10}{400}$$

e.m.f. in secondary
$$= \frac{10 \times 240}{400} \text{ (V)}$$
$$= 6 \text{ V}$$

(ii) With no energy loss:
power in primary = power in secondary
power = p.d. × current
∴ 240(V) × I = 6(V) × 4(A)
I = 0·1 A

Energy is lost as heating in the copper windings (coils) (I^2R).

Comment

Always quote the formula you use. This is the basic transformer equation, which you should know.

Remember: if no energy is lost then no power can be lost, as
$$\text{power} = \frac{\text{energy}}{\text{time}}$$

There are four main sources of energy loss:
(1) joule heating (I^2R) in the copper windings (coils),
(2) loss of magnetic flux between primary and secondary,
(3) hysteresis losses as the core reverses magnetism,
(4) heating due to eddy currents in the core.

Any one of these will do as an answer to the last part of the question.

Domestic Electricity Supply

Meaning of **peak voltage** and frequency of the domestic a.c. mains supply.
Advantages of **a.c. transmission** (also covered in last section with transformers).
Grid system; principles of the system and its advantages.
Electrical **safety**: fuses, earthing, colour coding for three-pin plugs.

Electricity and Magnetism 183

Kilowatt-hour as unit for **costing**, and simple problems on this.
Rectification: semi-conductor diode used as a rectifier in half-wave and bridge circuits, e.g. in a simple power unit; use of a capacitor as a reservoir for storage of charge.

Multiple Choice Questions

A popular form of question on these topics.

Question 1 (LON)
A kilowatt-hour of electrical energy is expended when

A a 50 W lamp is used for 2 hours
B an e.m.f. of 200 V maintains a steady current in a resistance of 100 Ω for fifteen minutes
C a current of 0·1 A is maintained in a resistance of 100 Ω for 10 hours
D a 3000 W heater is used for 20 minutes
E two 50 W lamps in parallel are operated on a 200 V supply for half an hour

Answer: D

To calculate kilowatt-hours, find $\dfrac{\text{no. of watts}}{1000} \times \text{no. of hours}$.

If you look quickly through the alternatives, you can see that **D** is the answer before bothering to work out more complicated systems like **E**.

Question 2 (AEB)
When a high voltage is connected to an electrical appliance, to what part of the appliance should the earth wire be connected?

A The positive terminal
B The negative terminal
C The casing
D The switch
E The fuse

Answer: C

You want to be safe when you touch the appliance, especially if there is a fault inside it!

Question 3 (AEB)
The correct colour code for wiring the flex of an electrical device to a 13 A three-pin plug is

	Live	Neutral	Earth
A	brown	blue	green/yellow
B	blue	green/yellow	brown
C	green/yellow	blue	brown
D	blue	brown	green/yellow
E	brown	green/yellow	blue

Answer: A

You should know this both to pass O-level and to be safe at home!

Question 4 (AEB multiple completion)
A suitable fuse is to be selected for an electrical appliance labelled 3 kW 250 V from fuses rated at 2A, 5A, 10A, 13A and 15A.

1 *The current carried by the appliance is 12 A.*	**Answer: 1** only Power = $V \times I$
2 *The most suitable fuse would be 10 A.*	$3000(W) = 250(V) \times I(A)$ $I = 12A$
3 *The resistance of the appliance is 12 Ω.*	∴ 10 A fuse would be too low.

$$R = \frac{V}{I} = \frac{250\,(V)}{12\,(A)} = 20\cdot 83\ \Omega$$

Longer Questions

Question 1 (AEB part question)
(a) When transmitting electrical energy from a power station to a consumer, state
  (i) why it is better to use a high voltage, and
  (ii) why it is better to use an a.c. voltage. *(4 marks)*
(b) A generator produces electrical power of 20 kW at 250 V. The generator is connected to a farm by cables of total resistance of 0·25 ohm. Calculate
  (i) the current in the cables, and
  (ii) the power loss in the cables. *(4 marks)*

Answer

(*a*) (i) A high voltage is used so that the power loss in the cables in the form of heat is as low as possible.

(ii) Alternating voltage is used so that transformers can be used to step up the voltage for transmission and step it down for normal use. Transformers work on changing magnetic flux and therefore need an alternating voltage.

(*b*) (i) Current = $\dfrac{\text{power}}{\text{p.d.}}$

= $\dfrac{20\,000(W)}{250(V)}$

= 80 A

Comment

These two questions are regularly asked about power transmission.

Remember: power = p.d. × current.

(ii) Power loss = I^2R
= 80 (A) × 80 (A) × 0·25 (Ω)
= 1600 W

Power loss is heating loss in the cables.

Question 2 (AEB)

(a) A correctly wired three-pin plug has the earth wire connected to the metal case of the appliance. A fuse is inserted in the plug.

(i) Why is it necessary to earth the appliance?
(ii) Why is a fuse necessary?
(iii) What colour is the earth lead? (6 marks)

(b) (i) Draw a circuit diagram of a simple power unit which is operated from the 240 V a.c. mains supply and produces a d.c. voltage of approximately 12 V.

(ii) State briefly the function of each of the electrical components in your circuit (10 marks)

(c) An electric fire, operated from the 240 V a.c. mains supply, is rated at 1·5 kW. When operating at rated power, calculate

(i) the current used by the fire,
(ii) the energy given out by the fire in 10 hours,
(iii) the cost of running the fire for 10 hours if the cost per kWh is 5p.
(9 marks)

Answer
(a) (i) It is necessary to **earth** the appliance in case the live wire should become connected to the metal case and so make it live.

(ii) A **fuse** is necessary so that, if a large current passes through the appliance, the fuse will blow rather than other parts of the appliance overheating (I^2R heating) and burning out.

(iii) The earth lead is yellow/green.

Comment
Earthing and use of *fuses* often appear in questions, so do learn about them.

(b) (i)

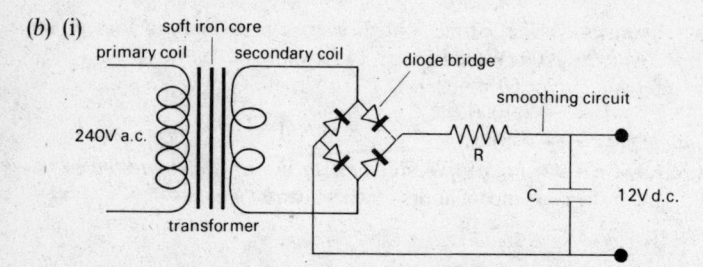

soft iron core
primary coil   secondary coil   diode bridge
smoothing circuit
240V a.c.
R
C   12V d.c.
transformer

(ii) The **transformer** steps down the a.c. mains voltage to the required 12 V. For an ideal transformer:

$$\frac{\text{primary e.m.f.}}{\text{secondary e.m.f.}} = \frac{\text{no. of turns in primary}}{\text{no. of turns in secondary}}$$

$$\therefore \frac{240\,(V)}{12\,(V)} = \text{turns ratio} = 20$$

The **diode bridge** rectifies the a.c. voltage as shown below.

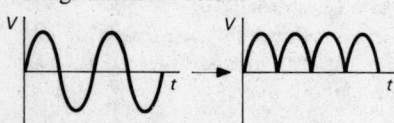

The **smoothing circuit** removes the *ripple effect* as shown below.

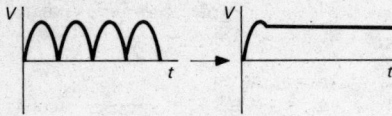

Three parts to this:
  transformer to step down the voltage,
  diode bridge to give full-wave rectification
  smoothing circuit to remove ripple.
Be sure your diagram shows these clearly, then say what you can about each part.
Diagrams (sketch graphs) may save you complicated explanations of what is happening.
Always quote formula.

(c) (i) Current = $\dfrac{\text{power}}{\text{p.d.}}$

$= \dfrac{1500\,(W)}{240\,(V)}$

$= 6\cdot 25$ A

Convert kW to W when substituting in formula.

(ii) Energy = power × time
    = 1500 (W) × 10
    × 60 × 60 (s)
    = 54 000 000 J
    (= 54 × 10⁶ J)

N.B. time in *seconds*.

(iii) No. of kWh = no. of kW × no. of hours
    = 1·5 × 10
    = 15
    ∴ cost = 15 × 5p
    = 75p

This is the only kind of problem where time is measured in *hours* rather than the usual seconds (SI unit).

Electrostatics

Charging by friction.
Attraction and repulsion. Positive and negative charge.
Charging by induction.
Structure and use of a **leaf-deflection electroscope** to show the presence of a charge and to determine its sign.
Electric fields.
Induction.
Action at a point: sparks; lightning; use of a Van de Graaff generator.
Use of capacitors and $Q = CV$ (JMB and OXF only).
Connection between current and static electricity.

Multiple Choice Questions

Question 1 (AEB)
A gold-leaf electroscope is given a negative charge so that the leaves are partially diverged. What happens to the leaves when a negatively charged body is brought near to the cap of the instrument? Do they

A collapse slowly?
B collapse immediately?
C remain as they are?
D diverge a little more?
E diverge a little less?

Answer: D
The speed of collapse would depend on the speed of bringing the charged body to the cap and this is not mentioned; so **A** and **B** can be discounted.

Question 2 (LON multiple completion)
A lightning conductor usually consists of thin pointed rods of conduction material. This is because

1 any charge on the conductor is concentrated at the points
2 the air near a pointed charged surface becomes ionized
3 electricity is more easily conducted along thin rods than along other shapes

Answer: 1, 2 only
Lightning conductors are often used as examples of electrostatic phenomena, so do learn about them.

Question 3 (AEB)
The capacitance of a parallel-plate capacitor depends on the

A area of overlap of the plates
B material of which the plates are made
C thickness of the plates
D charge on the plates
E potential difference between the plates

Answer: A
The capacitance of a capacitor is a property of its construction, so **D** and **E** can be rejected.
B and **C** are given as distractors since it is the material and thickness of the *space* between the plates which affects the capacitance.

Longer Questions

Question 1 (OXF)
Two metals spheres A and B each stand on an insulating base and are in contact. A negatively charged rod is brought near to the sphere A as shown in the diagram.

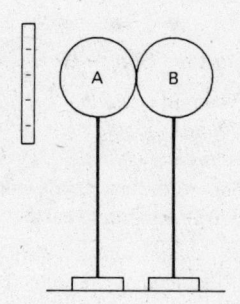

Electricity and Magnetism

(a) Explain in terms of electrons the difference between conductors and insulators. (2 marks)
(b) What effect does the charged rod have on electrons in A and B? Why? (2 marks)
(c) In what way will A and B differ if separated while the rod is near? (2 marks)
(d) How could the apparatus be used to leave A and B equally positively charged? (2 marks)
(e) How much if any of the charge on the rod is lost when the spheres are charged by induction? So how often could it be used to charge similar pairs of spheres without itself being recharged? (2 marks)

Answer

(a) In **conductors** the electrons are not firmly bound to their atoms, and can move freely from one atom to another. In an **insulator** the electrons *are* firmly bound to their atoms and will not move of their own accord.

(b) Since A and B are conductors, their electrons can move. They will be repelled from the side near the rod, which will be positively charged, and the far end will be negatively charged as shown.

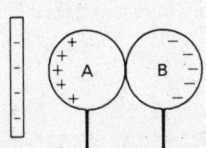

The insulating stands will stop the charge moving to earth.

(c)

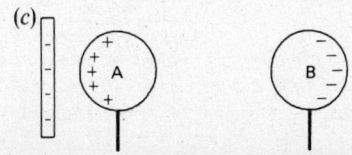

A and B will have opposite charges.

Comment

Only 2 marks, so spell out clearly the easiest difference. Don't go into great detail about the structure of the atom.

A diagram is essential, but for 'Why?' you will need some explanation, too.

This comment is probably not necessary, as only 2 marks are given.

Again, a diagram will be a great help (and will remind you what happens).

(d) If B is earthed, there will be a brief electron flow to earth. If the earth connection and then the charged rod are removed, A and B will be positively charged and the charge will spread equally over A and B.

(e) No charge is lost from the rod when the spheres are charged by induction, so it can be used to charge such spheres almost indefinitely without itself needing recharging.

This is the standard *charging by induction* technique.

Remember: *induced* charge is always opposite to the *inducing* charge.

If you don't know the answer this would be the sensible guess, since the question has no numbers in it at all.

Moving Charges

Ionization.
Identification of electric current with moving charge (see also 'Currents in circuits', pp. 163–70 and 'Electrostatics', pp. 187–90).
Conductors, insulators and semiconductors (see also 'Electrostatics', pp. 187–90).
Thermionic emission of electrons.
Properties of streams of electrons in vacuum, including magnetic and electrostatic **deflection**.
Cathode-ray oscilloscope (deflection system; use as a voltmeter, use of time base; traces obtained in simple d.c. and a.c. applications and their interpretations).

Multiple Choice Questions

Question 1 (OXF)

The indirectly heated diode valve contains two plates X and Y as shown in the diagram. A current will only cross the valve when plate X is

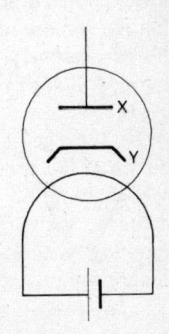

A raised to a high temperature
B connected to earth
C placed very close to plate Y
D made negative compared to plate Y
E made positive compared to plate Y

Answer: E
When Y is heated it gives off electrons by *thermionic emission*. These will only travel across the tube when X is positive compared to Y and attracts them.

Question 2 (A E B multiple completion)
The diagram shows the path of a beam of electrons deflected by a magnetic field in the region H, the field being perpendicular to the plane of the paper. The path would be more curved if

1 the field were stronger
2 the electrons were moving faster
3 the electrons were positively charged with an equal charge

Answer: 1 and 2 only
A change in the charge sign would mean a change in direction (Fleming's Left-hand Rule), not in the amount of curvature.

Question 3 (AEB)

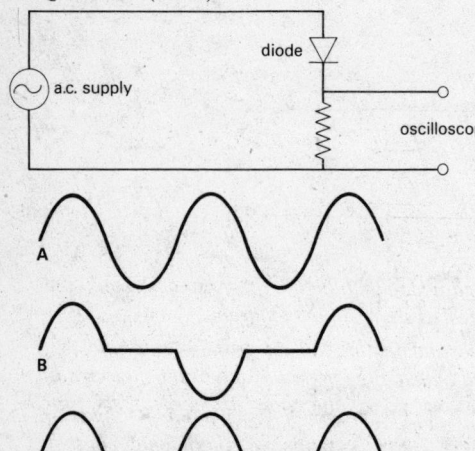

The Y-plates of a cathode-ray oscilloscope are connected across a resistance which is in series with a diode and an alternating-current supply as shown in the diagram. Which of the following patterns is produced on the screen of the oscilloscope?

Answer: C
The diode only allows current to pass through in one direction. During the other half-cycle it will be non-conducting and a straight line will be seen on the screen.

Electricity and Magnetism 193

Longer Questions

Question 1 (AEB)
(a)

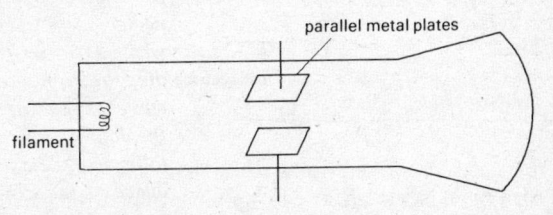

Two components of a simple cathode-ray tube are a tungsten filament and a pair of horizontal metal plates, as shown in the diagram.

(i) Name three other important features of the cathode-ray tube that would enable it to produce and indicate the presence of a beam of electrons.

(ii) Copy the diagram on your paper and show the positions of your three features.

(iii) How are electrons made to move along the tube?

(iv) Why is tungsten a good material for the filament? (8 marks)

(b) A modern cathode-ray oscilloscope has a set of plates called the Y-plates, like those shown in the diagram above, and a time base.

(i) What is the purpose of the time base?

(ii) What would be the trace seen on the screen when (1) a d.c. voltage, (2) an a.c. voltage is applied to the Y-plates, if in both cases the time base is switched off?

(iii) What would be the trace on the screen if a sensitive microphone were connected to the Y-plates, the time base being switched on, and (1) a vibrating tuning fork were placed in front of the microphone, or (2) a student sang into the microphone. (5 marks)

Answer

(a) (i) (1) An anode at a positive potential relative to the tungsten filament, with a hole for the electrons to pass through.

(2) A vacuum. (Alternatively: a pair of horizontal metal plates or a grid.)

(3) A fluorescent screen (or instead of a vacuum) a pair of horizontal metal plates or a grid).

Comment

'Name'; so don't bother to explain. No need for a beautiful diagram, but do label it very clearly.

(ii)

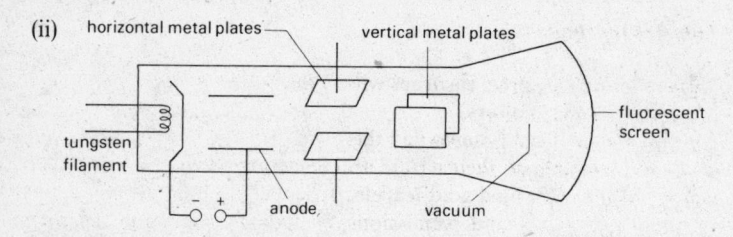

horizontal metal plates — vertical metal plates — fluorescent screen — tungsten filament — anode — vacuum

(iii) The electrons emitted from the tungsten filament are attracted to the anode and pass through it to the fluorescent screen.

Not many marks to spare for this, so it is probably only necessary to say that the electrons are attracted to the anode.

(iv) tungsten has a high melting point, so though it is heated it will not melt.

(b) (i) The time base makes the spot move across the screen slowly and then fly back, so that the variation of voltage with time can be studied.

There are only 5 marks available, and 5 parts of the question; probably one mark each, therefore.

(ii)

(1) d.c. just moves the spot up.

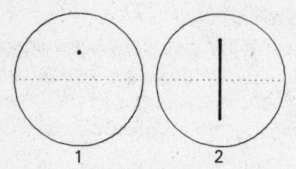

(2) Without the time base on, the trace would be 'squashed up' and would be a straight, vertical line.

(iii)

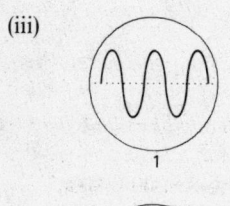

(1) The tuning-fork will vibrate to give a regular sine wave.

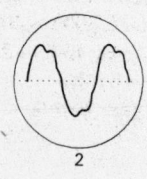

(2) The shape is not important, as long as you show that it repeats and that it is an irregular wave.

The Atom

Nucleus: proton, neutron; electrons within the atom.
Mass and **atomic numbers**.
Natural and artificial **isotopes** and their uses.
α-, β- and γ-**emissions**, their nature and detection by cloud chamber and Geiger–Müller tube (and gold-leaf electroscope; JMB only).
Properties of α-, β- and γ-emissions, including absorption in matter (shielding), mass and charge.
Understanding and use of simple **nuclear equations**.
Half-life: the time taken for half the atoms in any given sample of the substance to decay.

Multiple Choice Questions

These topics are often examined in multiple choice questions, several of which are therefore given here.

Question 1 (OXF)
(a) Which one of the following symbols represents a sodium atom containing 11 protons, 11 electrons and 12 neutrons?

A $^{11}_{22}Na$
B $^{12}_{11}Na$
C $^{22}_{12}Na$
D $^{23}_{11}Na$
E $^{34}_{11}Na$

Answer: D
The top number is the *mass number* = no. of protons + no. of neutrons. The bottom number is the *atomic number* = no. of protons.

Question 2 (AEB)
A radioactive source has an activity of 16 000 counts per minute. After 24 days the activity has fallen to 2000 counts per minute. After a further 8 days the likely activity, in counts per minute, is

A   0
B   250
C   500
D   1000
E   1500

Answer: D
One half-life: $16\,000 \rightarrow 8000$
Two half-lives: $8000 \rightarrow 4000$
Three half-lives: $4000 \rightarrow 2000$
∴ half-life = 8 days
∴ after another half-life:
$$2000 \rightarrow 1000$$

Question 3 (LON multiple completion)
The diagram represents the tracks produced when an alpha-source is used inside a cloud chamber.

From the diagram it may be concluded that
1 alpha-particles are positively charged
2 there is no strong magnetic field in the cloud chamber at right angles to the plane of the diagram
3 the range over which ionization occurs is the same for each particle

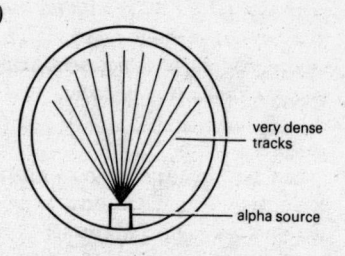

Answer: 2 and **3** only
Tracks emerge equally in all directions, so we have nothing to tell us about charge (although it is true that α-particles are positively charged).

Question 4 (LON matching pairs)
The following are five types of particles:

A alpha particles
B electron
C ion
D neutron
E proton

Which of these
(i) constitutes the nucleus of a hydrogen atom?
(ii) is emitted in β decay?
(iii) constitutes the nucleus of a helium atom?

(i) **Answer: E** Both the mass number and the atomic number of hydrogen is 1, so it has no neutrons and just one proton.
(ii) **Answer: B** You should know what α, β and γ emissions are.
(iii) **Answer: A** See comment above.

Longer Questions

Question 1 (LON part question)
The symbol for an atom of lead-210 is $^{210}_{82}Pb$.
What is the composition of the $^{210}_{82}Pb$ nucleus?
Lead-210 decays with the emission of a β-particle to form bismuth-210, which then decays with the emission of a β-particle to form polonium-210.

Polonium-210 decays with the emission of an α-particle to form lead. This can be shown as a series $^{210}_{82}Pb \xrightarrow{\beta} Bi \xrightarrow{\beta} Po \xrightarrow{\alpha} Pb$. Fill in, in the spaces above, the nucleon numbers and proton numbers for bismuth, polonium and lead in this decay series.

Answer
Mass no. (or nucleon no.) = no. of protons + no. of neutrons
Atomic no. = no. of protons
∴ for $^{210}_{82}Pb$
 no. of protons = 82
 no. of neutrons = 210 − 82
 = 128
$^{210}_{82}Pb \xrightarrow{\beta} {}^{210}_{83}Bi \xrightarrow{\beta} {}^{210}_{84}Po \xrightarrow{\alpha} {}^{206}_{82}Pb$

Comment
Remember, the top number is the mass (or nucleon) number, and the bottom number is the atomic number.

The emission of a beta-particle produces one fewer neutron in the nucleus and one extra proton. It is therefore equivalent to $_{-1}^{0}e$. The mass number is therefore unchanged, but the atomic number gains 1. An alpha-particle is a helium nucleus ($^{4}_{2}He$), and so the mass or nucleon number is reduced by 4 and the atomic number by 2.

Question 2 (LON)
(a) A Geiger–Müller tube attached to a scalar is placed on a bench in the laboratory. Over three consecutive minutes the scalar reads 11, 9, and 16 counts per minute. When a radioactive source is placed near to the Geiger–Müller tube the counts over three consecutive minutes are 1310, 1270 and 1296 per minute.
When a piece of thick paper is placed between the source and the tube the counts are 1250, 1242, and 1236 per minute.
When the paper is replaced by a sheet of aluminium 2 mm thick the counts are 13, 12 and 11 per minute.

   (i) Why is there a reading when no source is present? *(2 marks)*
   (ii) Why do the three readings in any one group differ? *(2 marks)*
   (iii) What can be deduced about the nature of the emission?
   Give reasons for your answer. *(5 marks)*

(b) What do you understand by the half-life of a radioactive element?
(2 marks)

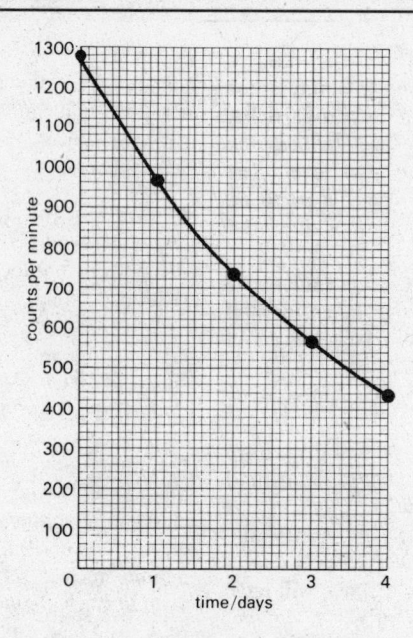

The graph above is plotted from readings taken with a radioactive source at daily intervals. Use the graph to deduce the half-life of the source.
(2 marks)
Hence, give the count rate after five days and the time when the count is 160 per minute. *(4 marks)*
Would you expect the mass of the source to have changed significantly after 4 days? Give a reason for your answer. *(3 marks)*

Answer	Comment
(a) (i) When no source is present, the Geiger–Müller tube records the **background count** which comes from active material in the earth and near-by surroundings, together with cosmic radiation from outer space.	Probably one mark for *background count* and one for the explanation.
(ii) The readings differ because **radioactive decay** is a **random** process and the number of counts is unlikely to be the same in consecutive minutes.	The word *random* is vital here.

(iii) Since thick paper reduces the average count per minute, some of the radiation must be **α-particles**. The aluminium sheet reduces the count to background level. The aluminium absorbs **β-particles**, therefore the emission is of α- and β-particles.

(b) The **half-life** of a **radioactive element** is the time taken for half the atoms in any given sample of the substance to decay.

The half-life of the source is $2\frac{1}{2}$ days.

After 5 days two half-lives have passed, therefore the count should be 320 counts/min.

The count will be 160 counts/min. after another half-life, i.e. $7\frac{1}{2}$ days.

After four days the mass will have changed significantly.

The proportion $\frac{420}{1280}, \simeq \frac{1}{3}$, will be remaining after 4 days.

Look at the materials used and consider what they absorb.

N.B. the final counts are nearly the same as the background, so at once you expect no γ-rays.

A definition to learn.

Initial reading is 1280 counts/min.; 640 counts/min. is at $2\frac{1}{2}$ days.
'5 days' in the question supports this answer for the half-life.

You do not know anything about what the source is decaying into, but notice that the question only asks about the *mass* of the source.

Question 3 (OXF)

Two parallel plates P, close together in air, are connected as shown in the diagram to a high-voltage d.c. supply S and a leaf electroscope. When a source of α-particles is placed at X, the air between the plates is ionized, and a small current flows.

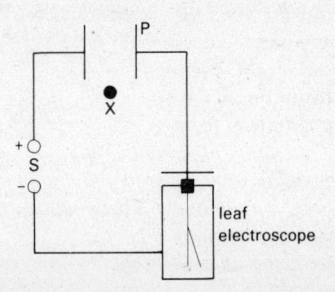

(i) Explain what 'ionized' means. *(3 marks)*
(ii) Why is air ionized by α-particles? *(2 marks)*
(iii) How does the leaf electroscope show that a current is flowing? *(2 marks)*
(iv) Why is there a current between the plates? *(2 marks)*
(v) What else (other than a radioactive source) could be used at X to produce the same effect? Explain *(2 marks)*

Answer

(i) **'Ionized'** means that the air is split into positive ions and electrons (ion pairs).

(ii) The α-particles (positively charged) are comparatively heavy and pull the electrons off the air atoms as they pass, thereby using their energy.

(iii) The leaf of the electroscope will pulse backward and forward at a rate which depends on the value of the ionizing current.

(iv) Because the plates are connected to the high-voltage d.c. supply there is an electric field between them, so as the ion pairs are formed the electrons are attracted to the positive plate and the positive ions to the negative plate. This movement of charged particles causes the current.

(v) A source of X-rays could be placed at X, as they also ionize air.

Comment

A simple explanation will do.

Remember: current = $\dfrac{\text{charge}}{\text{time}}$, so you expect the electroscope to change as current flows.

Remember: *current* is caused by the movement of *charged particles*.

You want something which will ionize air, and X-rays are the easiest choice.

General Questions

These appear less often for these subjects than for others, so fewer examples will be given.

Multiple Choice Questions

Question 1 (LON)
An example of a series of questions set on one practical situation.

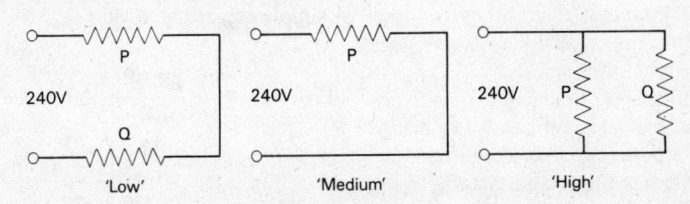

'Low'   'Medium'   'High'

P and Q represent two identical elements in an electric oven. Each element has resistance of 40 Ω when cold and 60 Ω under all operating conditions. By means of a suitable switch they may be connected in various ways as shown above. Normal operation is on 240 V mains.

(i) The maximum steady current which would be required under operating conditions is

A 12·0 A
B   8·0 A
C   6·0 A
D   3·0 A
E   2·0 A

Answer: B

Since $I = \dfrac{V}{R}$, the maximum current will be for the lowest resistance; in other words, for the parallel arrangement of the resistors. When operating, each element has a resistance of 60 Ω ∴ in parallel, total resistance $= \dfrac{R_1 \times R_2}{R_1 + R_2} = 30\ \Omega$

and $I = \dfrac{240\ (\text{V})}{30\ (\Omega)} = 8\cdot 0\ \text{A}$

(ii) In normal operation what is the minimum power-consumption of the oven?

A 8000 W
B 4000 W
C 1920 W
D 960 W
E 480 W

Answer: E

Power $= \dfrac{V^2}{R}$, so there will be minimum power when resistance is at its greatest, i.e. at 'Low'. Here, resistances are in series, so total resistance $= R_1 + R_2 = 120$.

$$\text{Power} = \frac{240(V) \times 240(V)}{120(\Omega)} = 480\,\text{W}$$

(iii) If the wire of element Q broke (i.e. it became open-circuited), the oven could be heated with the switch set

A to 'Medium' or 'Low'
B to 'Low' or 'High'
C to 'High' or 'Medium'
D only to 'Medium'
E in none of these positions

Answer: C

Q does not appear in 'Medium', so that would certainly be used. In 'High' the current could still flow through P even if Q were open-circuited.

(iv) If the supply voltage fell from 240 V to 230 V, the rate of supply of heat to the oven could change from H to (approximately)

A H (i.e. unchanged)
B $\left(\dfrac{230}{240}\right)^2 H$
C $\dfrac{230}{240} H$
D $\dfrac{240}{230} H$
E $\left(\dfrac{240}{230}\right)^2 H$

Answer: B

Power $= \dfrac{V^2}{R}$

$\therefore \dfrac{\text{power 2}}{\text{power 1}} = \dfrac{V_2^{\,2}}{V_1^{\,2}}$ (since R is unchanged)

$\qquad\qquad = \left(\dfrac{230}{240}\right)^2$

Question 2 (AEB multiple completion)
Electrical energy is converted into

1 light energy by means of a photo-electric cell
2 mechanical energy by means of a dynamo
3 sound energy by means of a loudspeaker

Answer: 3 only
Both **1** and **2** convert *into* electrical energy, not *from* it!

Longer Questions

Question 1 (AEB)
(a)

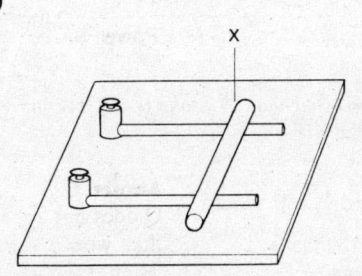

The diagram shows two pieces of bare wire connected to terminals on a piece of insulating material. A third piece of bare wire X rests on the wires and is free to move. You are given a number of dry cells, each of e.m.f. 1·5 V, and two bar magnets and are asked to use these to make the wire X move.

(i) How would you use the dry cells to produce a battery of 6 V?
(ii) Show by a diagram how you would use this battery and the magnets to make X move away from the terminals. *(5 marks)*

(b) The diagram shows a network of resistors.

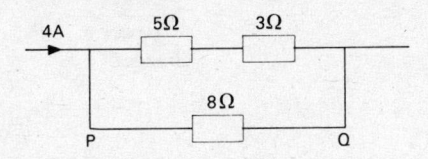

(i) If a current of 4 A enters the network as shown, what is the current in the branch PQ?
(ii) Calculate the voltage across the 5 Ω resistor. *(3 marks)*

(c) Draw a labelled diagram of a moving-coil loudspeaker and explain in detail how it works. *(7 marks)*

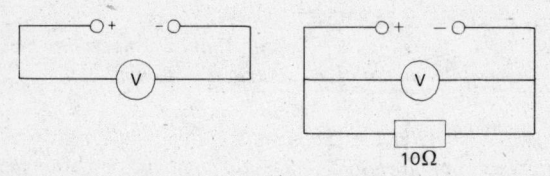

(d) The diagram shows two identical high-resistance voltmeters connected across two identical d.c. power sources. The left-hand voltmeter reads 6·0 V, but the right-hand voltmeter reads 4·0 V.

(i) Suggest why there is a difference between the readings of the two voltmeters.
(ii) What would be the reading on the voltmeter if the 10 Ω resistor were replaced by a 15 Ω resistor? *(6 marks)*

Answer
(a) (i) Four of the dry cells would be joined in series, as shown below.

Comment
In series: $E = E_1 + E_2 + E_3 + E_4$
and $6 = 4 \times 1·5$

(ii) N.B. magnets are at a right angle to X.

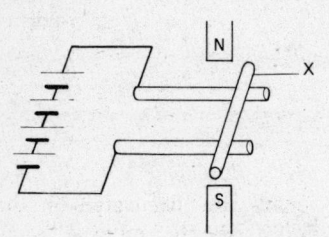

If you find it difficult to draw three-dimensional pictures, say the magnets are at a right-angle to X. Use Fleming's Left-hand Rule:

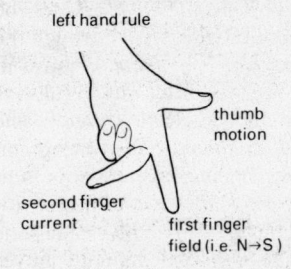

left hand rule

thumb motion

second finger current

first finger field (i.e. N→S)

Electricity and Magnetism 205

(b) (i)

[Circuit diagram: 4A entering at A, through 5Ω and 3Ω resistors to B; parallel branch P to Q with 8Ω resistor]

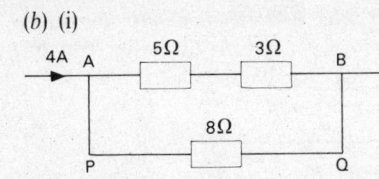

Since resistance AB = 5 Ω + 3 Ω = 8Ω, and as resistances are equal, current is split equally.
∴ current in PQ = 2 A

(ii) Since current through AB = 2 A
For 5 Ω resistor: $V = IR$
$= 2\,(A) \times 5\,(\Omega)$
$= 10$ V

It may help to redraw the diagram roughly.

Since it is the relationship between *resistances* in the two branches that is important, you need to work out R_{AB} *first*.

Quote formula.
Be careful to use *current* in top branch only.

(c)

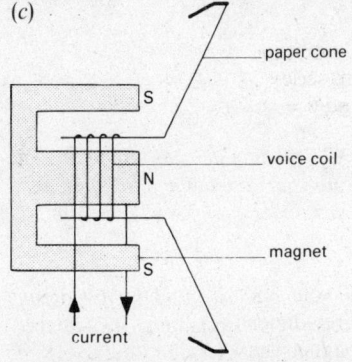

[Diagram of loudspeaker showing paper cone, voice coil, magnet with S-N-S poles, and current direction]

Varying electric currents corresponding to the sound to be reproduced are passed through the voice coil. This is free to move in the magnetic field, which is always at a right angle to the coil. The force on the current-carrying coil makes it move backwards and forwards in accordance with Fleming's Left-hand Rule; the cone (made of special material) moves with it and sets the surrounding air in vibration.

If your diagram is really clear, it will help your description below.

Explain why the charges in the current make the coil move backwards and forwards.

(d) (i) The left-hand voltmeter is reading the e.m.f. of the cell. The right-hand voltmeter is reading the p.d. across the 10 Ω resistor. In this case, the cell is delivering current and also doing work against the internal resistance.

The first diagram just measures e.m.f. so work out what the difference is in the second one.

(ii) From the left-hand diagram:
$E = 6·0$ V
In the right-hand diagram:
$$E = IR + Ir$$
$$I = \frac{V}{R}$$
$$\therefore E = V + \frac{V}{R}r$$
$$6·0 \, (V) = 4·0 \, (V) + \frac{4·0 \, (V)}{10 \, \Omega} r \, (\Omega)$$
$$r = 5 \, \Omega$$
For the new situation:
$$E = V + \frac{V}{R}r$$
now $R = 15 \, \Omega$:
$$6·0 \, (V) = V \, (V) + \frac{V \, (V)}{15 \, (\Omega)} \times 5 \, (\Omega)$$
$$= V + \frac{V}{3} = \frac{4V}{3}$$
$$V = 4·5 \text{ V}$$

This part obviously needs to use the numbers given in the question. You should know the whole circuit formula $E = IR + Ir$.

Use the first information to find the internal resistance, and then substitute for the second situation.

MORE ABOUT PENGUINS, PELICANS, PEREGRINES AND PUFFINS

For further information about books available from Penguins please write to Dept EP, Penguin Books Ltd, Harmondsworth, Middlesex UB7 0DA.

In the U.S.A.: For a complete list of books available from Penguins in the United States write to Dept DG, Penguin Books, 299 Murray Hill Parkway, East Rutherford, New Jersey 07073.

In Canada: For a complete list of books available from Penguins in Canada write to Penguin Books Canada Limited, 2801 John Street, Markham, Ontario L3R 1B4.

In Australia: For a complete list of books available from Penguins in Australia write to the Marketing Department, Penguin Books Australia Ltd, P.O. Box 257, Ringwood, Victoria 3134.

In New Zealand: For a complete list of books available from Penguins in New Zealand write to the Marketing Department, Penguin Books (N.Z.) Ltd, Private Bag, Takapuna, Auckland 9.

In India: For a complete list of books available from Penguins in India write to Penguin Overseas Ltd, 706 Eros Apartments, 56 Nehru Place, New Delhi 110019.